instruments of unity

instruments of unity

National Councils of Churches
within the One Ecumenical Movement

Edited by Thomas F. Best

WCC Publications

Cover design: Edwin Hassink

ISBN 2-8254-0936-7

© 1988 WCC Publications, World Council of Churches,
150 route de Ferney, 1211 Geneva 20, Switzerland

Printed in Switzerland

Contents

Preface

The most ecumenical meeting ever held was probably that of 120 representatives of some 70 national councils of churches (NCCs) who gathered at the Ecumenical Centre in Geneva, 20-24 October 1986. The consultation, sponsored by the World Council of Churches, also included representatives from regional conferences of churches. During the period between this meeting and the earlier world consultation of national councils of churches in 1971, the family of NCCs had grown enormously. And among these councils, the Roman Catholic Church had taken on full membership in one-third of the now 90 national councils. This was, indeed, an important ecumenical meeting.

The programme was developed in active consultation with the NCCs themselves. It was based on issues which the councils themselves wanted to pursue, on concerns which sprang from their own life and witness. These issues, grouped around five themes, provided the central matters for discussion in workshops in the following areas: ecclesiological issues; the role of NCCs in promoting ecumenism; mission and dialogue; finance, service/development, and resource sharing; and councils in their social and political context. You will find the reports of those discussions within these pages.

Into the workshop discussions came also matters raised in Bible studies and plenary presentations, stories and exchanges of experience within regional meetings, plenary debates and solidarity actions.

The week was intense and the encounter rich. Special thanks are due to General Secretary Allan Kirton of the Caribbean Conference of Churches, who chaired the steering committee; to Jocelyn Armstrong and Eustace Renner, leaders of the national ecumenical bodies of New Zealand and Sierra Leone respectively, who were plenary moderators; to Fr Hervé

Legrand for his presentation on "Councils of Churches as Instruments of Unity within the One Ecumenical Movement"; and to Jean Skuse who spoke on "The Councils Serving the Churches in Their Mission of Justice, Peace and Service to the World". Gratitude must be expressed, too, for the cooperation of colleagues from the Secretariat for Promoting Christian Unity, especially Msgr Basil Meeking and Sister Joan Delaney. And there must be a general word of thanks to the many staff members of the WCC who planned and facilitated the programme activities. Their final contribution to the future of the work among and between NCCs is found in Appendix 2 of this book, a list of councils which we believe to be the most up-to-date and accurate available. There you will find the addresses of people who made the consultation an occasion of praise, prayer, biblical study, song, laughter and learning.

The ecumenical movement moves, it would seem, by means of a small boat. It is powered by neither oars nor engines, and seems to be without crew or captain — if the logo of the ecumenical movement can be believed. Hardly what one would choose to board for a voyage of discovery! But when seventy such boats were lashed together for five or six days in October 1986, each of them with its captain and crew, with the wind blowing strong and the waves lashing the shore, the movement moved and there were discoveries aplenty.

RUTH SOVIK

The Second NCC Consultation: the Issues and the Experience

MARLIN VANELDEREN

"Master, we toiled all night and took nothing!"

People working ecumenically are sometimes tempted to think that Simon Peter's terse summary of a nocturnal fishing expedition (Luke 5:5) offers a fairly accurate assessment of their own efforts. That sobering observation came from Allan Kirton, general secretary of the Caribbean Conference of Churches, in a sermon at the worship service opening a meeting of representatives of national councils of churches, held at the Ecumenical Centre in Geneva, 20-24 October 1986.

The factors Kirton said contribute to this sort of malaise were familiar to his listeners. How can the vision and enthusiasm that fuel a "movement" survive institutionalization and, some would say, bureaucratization? How can councils of churches cope with widespread suspicion of and even attacks on what they are and do? How can they live on support from member churches that is at best sporadic? How can they compete with the ideology of the "new right" that so many Christians find alluring these days?

As Kirton said, it's enough to drive some ecumenists to self-pity and withdrawal from the fray, some to scape-goating and mutual recriminations, some to fish for solutions in the murkier waters of dogmatic theology and ecclesiology — and all of us, perhaps, to that great ecumenical illusion that we can get rid of our problems by talking them to death.

But if there were hints of all these temptations during the Geneva meeting, the encounter for the most part achieved its aim: to offer a forum in which persons from national councils of churches could share how they are facing their common and unique problems, could reflect on what their role in the ecumenical movement is today and might be tomorrow, could come to a new understanding of each other's struggles and could deepen their commitments to work and pray with one another.

I. The meeting and the participants

More than 120 people (representing about 70 of the world's approximately 90 national councils of churches) took up the invitation of the World Council of Churches to attend the consultation. Fifteen years had passed since the only other world consultation of representatives of national councils of churches (attended by only half as many people). Since mid-1971, many new councils have come into existence, and the number of councils in which the Roman Catholic Church holds full membership has more than trebled (from 10 to 33; Roman Catholics have "observer" status in seven other NCCs, besides membership in the regional ecumenical organizations of the Caribbean and the Pacific).

With these developments in view, and a sense that the challenges facing Christian councils have changed over the years, the WCC Central Committee in 1984 recommended that a second world consultation of NCCs be convened "on the initiative of the WCC and in appropriate collaboration with the Roman Catholic Church".

Some NCCs are "associated councils", formally related to the WCC and entitled to send delegates to its Assemblies and Central Committee meetings. Others — "affiliated councils" — relate to the WCC's Commission on World Mission and Evangelism but for one reason or another do not choose to become directly associated with the WCC as a whole. A third category is Christian councils "in working relationship" with the WCC — often functioning as a channel of communication and cooperation with the WCC's Commission on Inter-Church Aid, Refugee and World Service.

Inviting the cooperation of the Roman Catholic Church in planning the 1986 consultation was logical. Since 1972, the NCC issue has been on the agenda of the Joint Working Group (JWG) between the Roman Catholic Church and the WCC.

An early fruit of these discussions was the 1975 publication by the Vatican Secretariat for Promoting Christian Unity (SPCU) of a pamphlet on "Ecumenical Collaboration at the Regional, National and Local Levels" (see Appendix 1). While emphasizing the limitations on the competence and authority of local and national councils of churches, and pointing out that national or regional bishops' conferences must decide for or against membership according to their own particular context, not some general rule made in Rome, the SPCU document is generally positive towards national councils.

"Among the many forms of ecumenical cooperation, councils of churches and Christian councils are not the only form," the document says, "but they are certainly one of the more important"; and it welcomes "the responsible contacts which the Catholic Church is having with them".

The JWG noted in 1979 that "a common assessment of the role of regional and national councils, especially in terms of collaboration with the Roman Catholic Church, would be a particularly useful contribution to the clarification of 'the way to unity'". Following that call, a joint consultation was held in February 1982 in Venice, sponsored by the SPCU and the WCC Faith and Order Commission.

*   *   *

But what are these bodies whose representatives came to the Geneva meeting? Some hint of the rich diversity subsumed under the term "national councils of churches" came from self-portraits in plenary sessions, printed literature and photographs displayed at information tables, comments made in informal conversations and replies to questions.

They are large and small — in terms of number of member churches, number of staff, size of budget. Some seem to be thriving; others to be plodding along; still others are obviously struggling. Their origins vary, though many can be traced back to the missionary movement. What their constituency expects of them ranges widely — from not much of anything in some cases to the clearly impossible in others. How they see their own role is linked to their assessment of the society and government of their country (and to the attitude of that society and government towards churches).

A few examples illustrate some of the challenges.

• Anezka Ebertova spoke of Czechoslovakia as a context in which ecumenical understanding is still at an early stage. "In the past our churches have had to struggle for their identity," she said, "so they have been less open to cooperation." And the Czech Ecumenical Council has only part-time volunteer staff.

• C. F. Beyers Naudé, general secretary of the South African Council of Churches until his retirement in 1987, portrayed the deeply divided Christian community in his country. The SACC's 15 member churches represent 12 million of the country's 26 million Christians: the three powerful white Dutch Reformed Churches are not members, nor are the Baptist, Pentecostal and many African Independent churches.

Restrictions imposed by the apartheid regime sometimes oblige the SACC to act illegally, Naudé said, but if the church were not willing to face the possibility of becoming disobedient to the state, it would never give a meaningful witness to the people in their struggle for liberation and peace. And so, despite the laws, the SACC has appealed to the outside world to support sanctions against South Africa and has undertaken to build up contacts with liberation movements, without whom there can be no political solution for the country.

Speaking with a united voice is difficult for the SACC, given the different theological views among its constituency on issues like violence and non-violence, the concept of reconciliation, opposition to unjust government and deciding at what point the church must declare that it no longer recognizes the government as legitimate.

• It isn't only in South Africa itself that much of the agenda for the national council of churches is set by apartheid. In Tanzania, for example, the Christian Council devotes considerable energy to dealing with the plight of thousands of refugees who have fled South Africa.

• One of the older bodies represented at the meeting was the French Protestant Federation. Created in 1908, after the separation of church and state in France, to maintain links between Protestant churches for common witness and to defend the interests of French Protestantism, it has since broadened to include Pentecostal churches as well as a variety of Protestant institutions and movements. It is responsible for a radio and television ministry in its deeply secularized country, and serves as a spokesman for the churches. (A major issue on the federation's agenda — creation of a national council of churches in the country — was realized in December 1987 with the constitutive assembly of the Council of Christian Churches in France.)

• Like many others, the NCC in Bangladesh, according to Michael Adhikari, cannot be understood apart from the familiar story of European colonialism hand-in-glove with Christian mission. Just as the colonial powers and traders — Portuguese, Spanish, French, Danish, Dutch and English — fought among themselves, so too the missions were divided, struggling for sectoral superiority. While Hindus were moving towards being able to worship at the same shrine, and all Muslims could enter the same mosque, "Christians were marked by refusal to participate in common worship and growing separation and diversity", Adhikari says.

The end of British rule, the partition in 1947 of India and Pakistan (the latter predominantly Muslim state divided into two parts separated by hundreds of kilometres), and the subsequent liberation of Bangladesh (formerly East Pakistan) in 1971, brought developments that had critical consequences for the ecumenical movement in Bangladesh.

For one thing, 80 percent of the educated Christians of East Bengal lived around Calcutta — and did not opt for East Pakistan with the partition. Under the circumstances of need, all the Protestant communities of East Pakistan joined together to form the East Pakistan Christian Council in 1949. For a time, it seemed, long-standing rifts between churches were being healed. But an ominous sign of problems to come took place in the early 1960s, when the Assemblies of God mission was told by its US headquarters to sever ties with the EPCC. The local Assemblies of God congregations followed suit.

When the EPCC became the NCC Bangladesh in 1971, it also changed its organization. Reflecting the spirit of political independence that had given birth to the country, the NCC recognized only denominations as members, giving the missions a role in the background.

But around the time of liberation, over a dozen new missions entered Bangladesh — all of them zealous, in the new situation, "to convert all Bangladeshis", Adhikari says. These groups, not affiliated with the national councils in their own countries, were anxious to form an "evangelical" grouping in Bangladesh.

At the same time, churches abroad were sending a vast amount of money and material aid into the newly created and war-torn country. Because the NCC was unable to cope with this influx, Adhikari says, "the agencies started operating directly through their own representatives" and "new leaders grew up with foreign funding". Not only did these groups stay outside the NCC but started what Adhikari describes as "a campaign of hostility against it".

In conclusion, "the bond of brotherhood between various churches and missions has been weakening gradually. As a result, the power of understanding the dimension of Christianity that transcends geographical boundaries is lost. Bangladesh is a glaring example of the result of division of the churches."

Other participants offered self-portraits in the concrete form of a specific appeal for assistance or solidarity from their fellow-councils.

• A delegate from Japan asked other NCCs to write letters to the Japanese ambassador in their country protesting the way foreigners living in Japan are treated — symbolized by the requirement (especially directed against Koreans) that they be finger-printed.

• African participants proposed creation of an ecumenical solidarity fund to help the frontline states bordering on South Africa to respond to the needs of apartheid's victims.

• A Philippines ecumenical leader, reminding others of the monumental problems facing his country even after the overthrow earlier in 1986 of Ferdinand Marcos, asked for "a new international political consensus that small struggling nations seeking selfhood should have the right to be masters of their land and creators of their own history".

The consultation was not insulated from the world outside. Scarcely had it begun when news reports came in of the airplane crash that took the life of Mozambique's president Samora Machel. A meditation at a memorial service organized by African participants asked: "Why must the people of Mozambique suffer again and again? But God does not abandon us. God does not abandon his people. God does not abandon the people of Mozambique... The churches must not, the churches cannot give up mission and service tasks in this drifting world... We are responsible for the mourning people of Mozambique. We are in solidarity with the long struggle for justice and peace, because this is God's fight." Participants also sent a letter to the prime minister of Mozambique, asking him to convey their condolences to the people of the country.

For many who took part, what went on outside of the scheduled sessions — opening and closing worships, morning Bible studies, plenary papers and discussions, a choice of workshops on five topics, sharing encounters in 15 small groups — was as significant as what is recorded in the reports drafted by the meeting. Particularly because it had been so long since such a meeting had been held — and only a handful of participants at the 1986 meeting had been present fifteen years earlier — the planning of the meeting was designed to maximize opportunities for informal conversations.

As usually happens, the shortness of available time in a five-day meeting (when many participants are exhausted by travel from great distances) and the scope of the agenda limited the possibilities for unshackling people from a tight schedule. Everyone agreed that the agenda was full; some thought it was too crowded and the objectives in terms of reporting were too ambitious, especially after seeing how little time there actually was to discuss (and receive by consensus) documents drafted by the workshops. Others found the week's structure too "traditional" and/or too "Western".

Despite the high percentage of positive responses to the WCC invitation, some pointed to groups who were absent from or under-represented in the deliberations: Orthodox churches especially, but also urban rural mission groups, action groups, "minjung churches", basic Christian communities. One national council of churches was unrepresented at the meeting through no fault of its own: authorities in South Korea refused an exit visa to NCCK general secretary Kim So Young.

A half dozen "letters of solidarity" were drafted for participants to sign as a way to express their sharing of the concerns of churches and councils in Chile, Korea, Namibia, Nicaragua, South Africa and Sri Lanka. Although these were not "official" documents to be "adopted" by the meeting, discussion of their contents was lively. The Nicaragua letter typified the ambiguity of trying to channel solidarity through parliamentary decision-making procedures. One participant felt that mention in the letter of "counter-revolutionaries sponsored by a foreign power" was too weak: "Why don't we say who we are talking about?" Another feared that addressing a messsage of support only to the Protestant interchurch aid committee (Nicaragua has no national council of churches) might deepen the gap between Catholics and Protestants in the country. In the end it was decided that participants should sign the letters as they were — either as individuals or as representatives of their own council — but that no editing of the drafts would be undertaken by the meeting.

II. Fostering ecumenical relationships

Not surprisingly, ecumenical relationships were a major theme of the discussions during the meeting.

Calling the consultation was a response by the WCC to a mandate from the Sixth Assembly: *"fostering ecumenical relationships* with and between churches, communities, groups and ecumenical organizations on all levels should become a priority for the WCC".

The Assembly, alluding to its own theme, had noted: "Jesus Christ is the life of the world. This life is to be expressed through maturing ecumenical relationships among the churches... New ecumenical relationships should be nurtured locally and regionally... Existing relationships should be renewed and sustained..."

1. Relating to member churches

The most visible relationship for an NCC, of course, is that between the council and its member churches.

In its rarefied theological form, the issue of how an NCC relates to member churches is the question of the "ecclesial nature of the council". The presence at the meeting of Roman Catholic participants and representatives of NCCs with Roman Catholic membership ensured that this topic received due attention, particularly in the paper by Hervé Legrand and in one of the workshops.

Which is not to say that everyone was equally convinced of the significance of the "ecclesiological significance" discussion. Some, in fact, impatiently dismissed it as another case of churches from the North taking refuge in classical theological hair-splitting from the real issues of poverty, injustice and systemic oppression. Are any local congregations seriously exercised by the question of the ecclesial nature of the NCC, an Asian participant wondered aloud. Doesn't this sort of high-powered theologizing give them the feeling that the whole ecumenical process bypasses them?

One could argue that this response merely poses the same question in less formal terms. For Christians at the local level to judge that the national council of churches in the country is setting its agenda without reference to its "grassroots" constituents is not much different from claiming that the council has arrogated too much "ecclesial significance" to itself.

In fact, suggested Arie Brouwer, general secretary of the US National Council of Churches, there is sometimes a tendency in the churches to use the "ecclesial significance" argument as a way of reining in an NCC's engagement in society. Brouwer worried that insistence that an NCC not go beyond its explicit mandate may hinder it — and the churches — from "catching up to where the Spirit has already led us".

But there were clearly diverging emphases on this question of the role of the NCC. Some comments and group reports accented the element of being an instrument in the service of member churches. "The first priority for the NCC", in the words of the report of one of the small groups, "is to serve its member churches". An NCC official from an African country described his own organization as the "handmaiden" of the member churches.

Others warned against construing the relationship of service in a way that reduces the NCC to a mere robot of the churches. C.O. Williams of Nigeria argued that "the more self-reliant a council is, the better it is for the member churches". David Gill of the Australian Council of Churches insisted that any services an NCC undertakes for its member churches should aim at helping them to become more ecumenical. Donald Anderson of the Canadian Council of Churches echoed that: "We must be a place that helps all our member churches model what we are to become — even if we don't know very clearly what that is!" Councils, Anderson said, must keep pushing, dreaming, going beyond what the churches have identified as their common agenda.

But talk of "creative tensions" with member churches, of the need to "push" them, of the challenges that a council's prophetic stance may pose to its member churches was balanced by the realization that the relationship between the council and its member churches must be close. NCCs have to understand the reality of their churches. If a national council has a weak relationship with what one small group called "the main denominational church life in the country", the work of that council will be limited. Ecumenism is already a low priority for many churches; and there would seem to be little future for a national council which reflects the concerns of only a shrinking and marginalized coterie of ecumenical specialists.

A council's readiness to offer services does not necessarily mean its member churches will welcome or support these. In Liberia, for example, said Imogene Collins, the churches are much older than the NCC, and many of their programmes have existed for a long time and — thanks to strong historical and confessional links with churches elsewhere — are assured of funding. Thus, the churches' own activities take priority over any programmes the national council may decide to undertake.

Gabriel Habib of the Middle East Council of Churches pointed out that those who concentrate on the council's service to member churches often think of service in a very narrow sense as only aid and development. But when a council puts all its eggs into this basket, neglecting such important services as education, theological study, evangelism and dialogue, Habib warned, groups from outside the ecumenical fellowship may fill the vacuum thus left, exacerbating the existing divisions among the churches.

2. The issue of Roman Catholic membership

Is the question of relationships with member churches qualitatively different in cases where Roman Catholics are NCC members? Some participants thought so; but it was clear that the experiences were sufficiently diverse to warn against generalizing.

A number of representatives observed that it is by no means the case within a council that the same churches will always line up on the same side of every issue. In the Federal Republic of Germany, for example, the Roman Catholics join with the Lutherans on some issues, with the "free churches" on others.

As the SPCU document explains at some length, Roman Catholics have difficulties with the practice of some councils of making public statements on issues of common concern. In the Netherlands, for example, where the ethical question of euthanasia has engendered widespread public controversy in the last several years, discussions in the council of churches about making a statement on it were complicated because the Roman Catholic bishops were bound to authoritative Catholic moral teaching on the issue.

When the Canadian Catholic bishops became associate members of the Canadian Council of Churches, Donald Anderson said, the CCC rewrote its bylaws to accommodate "opting out" of statements by a single member church. But in New Zealand, it was observed, such a "dissent clause" had existed long before there was any talk of Roman Catholic participation — to respect the sensibilities of the Salvation Army.

Representatives from a number of countries said Roman Catholics take a more active ecumenical role on the national scene, including collaboration in addressing social issues, than Protestant churches, especially those who are "conservative evangelical". Those who attested to this experience said collaboration in common worship and theological discussion is often more difficult to achieve than working together in society.

In Namibia, one participant suggested, the absence of a financial base to support ecumenical theology is a major factor here, as it is in many other areas of the third world. Laurentius Klein of Germany expressed hope that this would change as, he said, the Roman Catholic Church becomes more and more a "third-world church", with more than half of the bishops now coming from those parts of the world.

Others accented the complementarity within an NCC that includes Roman Catholic membership. As the Workshop I report puts it, the Roman Catholic Church as a world communion can inspire the national council of churches to be more ecumenical, while the national churches in the NCC can inspire the Roman Catholic Church to be more locally oriented. Or, in the words of W. van der Zee of the Council of Churches in the Netherlands, "the Protestant churches ask the Roman Catholics, 'Is national pluriformity possible?' and the Roman Catholics ask the Protestants, 'Do you realize that you are part of a world church?'"

But getting to the point where learning from each other's strengths is possible presupposes that Roman Catholic authorities in the country are aware of the importance of national councils of churches, for, as the SPCU document says, it is ultimately their responsibility "to decide on the acceptability and the appropriateness of all forms of local ecumenical action". That isn't always the case, participants were told. Some Roman Catholic bishops seem to be unfamiliar with the SPCU guidelines on ecumenical collaboration — or even the Decree on Ecumenism of the

Second Vatican Council. One thing that is needed, it was agreed, is for news of positive experiences of Roman Catholic participation in NCCs to be disseminated more widely.

At the same time, non-Roman Catholic churches must be willing to respect the self-understanding of the Roman Catholic Church — and that is by no means always the case either. Of course, the ecumenical situation may be blocked if the Roman Catholic self-understanding leads them to refuse to become involved in an NCC because they believe this would somehow put all the churches on an unwarrantedly equal footing.

But Kenyon Wright of the Scottish Churches' Council argued that there is a sense in which the hesitation or reluctance of some Roman Catholics to become involved in an NCC can be seen as a "gift": a token of unwillingness to consent too easily to the denominationalism which so many other churches accept without question.

3. What role for non-member churches?

Another category of NCC relationships with churches in its country touched on was how NCCs relate to churches which — because of either their relatively small size or their decision not to affiliate with the NCC — have little influence on what it is or does.

The presence of churches which are not NCC members highlights a tension in the self-understanding of any NCC between *comprehensiveness* — a desire to include the broadest possible spectrum of Christian groups and churches — and *focus* — a desire to foster a clear vision of what ecumenism requires and to live out that vision in common undertakings.

Some churches may stay outside of the NCC in their country simply because they have other priorities and have not come to see the importance of ecumenism. Conceivably, collaboration in interchurch events at a local level, personal contacts, continuing information about the positive benefits of ecumenical fellowship may open such groups to eventual application for council membership.

A greater concern for NCCs is with non-member churches who take a negative, even adversarial stance towards the council. Often they keep up a barrage of accusations against the council — typically charging it with infidelity to the gospel and unsavoury political allegiances. And in many cases they work to set up their own alternative "ecumenical" structures.

Many of these non-member groups and churches fall under the widely (if not always precisely) used category of "conservative evangelical". Rupert Young of Jamaica urged that the issue of relations with conservative evangelicals is in fact as important for NCCs as that of their ties with Roman Catholics.

Sometimes the paradoxical situation arises that the NCC itself becomes an obstacle to ecumenism. In Liberia, said Imogene Collins, many churches are far more inclined to do something together with other churches if it *isn't* undertaken under the banner of the NCC.

The minority-majority church question is also a tricky one. When a national council includes a church whose membership accounts for the overwhelming majority of the country's Christian population, how can it avoid being so dominated by that church as to smother any ecumenical initiatives it might take?

Workshop I, acknowledging the difficulties that majority-minority situations create, urged that formation of an NCC under such circumstances is both advantageous and difficult.

The problem is not necessarily one of ill will. In Ireland, David Bleakley noted, with the vast majority of its population Roman Catholic, the NCC would be overwhelmed if the Catholics were to join. "They're embarrassed by that and so are we," he said.

The question of "proportional representation" may not quite be the heart of the issue here — after all, much of what NCCs do is undertaken without voting being necessary or even appropriate — though it does serve as a useful symbol of the difficulty. But as in any "power issue", no easy solution is apparent.

In some countries with a majority-minority church situation, the ecumenical atmosphere is clouded by charges of proselytism. When that issue was aired at the meeting, all the familiar points of tension surfaced: from the one side, charges that those who seek converts from among members of another Christian church are usually blinded by their zeal into violating the very human rights of those whom they seek to convert and their families; from the other side, charges that it is often the majority church, in many cases a "folk church" or a "state church", which is violating the rights both of the minority church — by falsely portraying its fidelity to the gospel's evangelistic call as something heretical and illegal — and of its own members — whose religious freedom is infringed by any effort to deny them the opportunity to change their religion.

A mediating position, which some articulated, recognizes that proselytism can be a sinister and destabilizing force in society, but that majority churches ought to consider seriously and self-critically what the attractiveness of other churches says about their own weakness.

The problem of proselytism would not be solved at this meeting, it was clear. And David Gill advised against spending too much time trying to define what proselytism is. The important point to make as far as NCCs are concerned, he suggested, is that "wherever there is a point of tension like this, it should be a priority for the ecumenical structure to address that problem".

4. Relations with other religious groups

Discussion of relations between NCCs and religious groups in their country who would not ordinarily be classified as "churches" touched on three categories of such groups: less structured groups of Christians, such as base communities and action groups, especially those involving marginalized people in the society; para-church organizations from abroad; and people of other faiths, including adherents of "new religious movements".

Several participants suggested that one of the vocations of an NCC is to give marginalized groups in the country — whether within or outside of the churches — space to develop their identity. At the same time, as Jocelyn Armstrong of the NCC in New Zealand warned, any effort to move beyond rhetoric to give actual access to those who have been marginalized will create fear in many of those who have previously been exercising the power.

That's bound to be a problem if an NCC member church has the impression that the council is paying more attention to a certain group or faction within that church than to its official "leadership", especially if that group and the leadership are dramatically at odds. (This is, of course, an ecumenical problem that is hardly limited to NCCs.)

It's also complicated if the marginalized Christian group does not understand itself (or no longer understands itself) as affiliated with an institutional church. With all the talk about ecumenism as more than "interchurch relations", with the realization (as one small group put it) that NCCs must "seek new allies", including those who do not profess Christian faith, in their work for justice, it clearly won't do to exclude Christian groups — especially those whose commitment to justice is passionate and radical — from ecumenical participation just because they don't look or act like most churches.

At the same time, warnings were sounded against the siren song of ideologies. One workshop report accented the need for NCCs to help churches "keep their identity" when they seem ready to buy into an ideology, saying that a sober and critical attitude *vis-à-vis* ideologies is needed if a church is to retain its prophetic ministry.

The ideological threat that seemed uppermost in the minds of most participants was that of the "new right", particularly as it manifests itself in countries of the South, where it is imported through "conservative evangelical" agencies from abroad (usually North America or Western Europe).

Sang Jung Park, general secretary of the Christian Conference of Asia, sketched a grim picture of two different forms of the religious right ideology which are infiltrating many Asian countries where Christian communities are small minorities. One says: "There are 2 billion people on this continent. If we don't bring every one of them into the church quickly, communism is going to take over the world." The other group, more apocalyptic, says: "This world is hopeless. The only way out is to generate conflict between the super-powers, so that it will all come to an end." Groups like these are growing, Park said, because of their access to vast amounts of money and their skill and sophistication in the use of the media.

A sad by-product of para-church operations is the divisions they foster among Christians, especially damaging to a minority Christian community, creating a scandal far removed from the real scandal of the gospel. As one participant asked, how can Christians credibly dialogue with people of other faiths when our own house is so divided?

Others urged recognition that it is a reaction against secularism which turns many people to these para-church groups from outside. Some described them as a Christian parallel to Islamic fundamentalism, which is also often fed by fear or anger at seeing what was once perceived as the common religious basis of society eroded. Apart from identifying the destructive influence these groups may exert, therefore, there was also talk of the need for a serious re-evangelization of what used to be called "Christendom".

Ideological considerations aside, the flow and use of outside resources creates major problems for national churches in third-world countries. The influx from missions makes it difficult for us to act, said Michael Adhikari of Bangladesh, because in third-world countries power is in the hands of the military and of those who have money. Similarly, Max Rafransoa of the All Africa Conference of Churches noted that in Kenya alone, where the AACC is headquartered, "there are 400 separate organizations — 100 of them para-church groups — working to save the country. What they do in fact is to perpetuate the crisis."

Perhaps the most controversial discussions of the entire week were in the workshop on mission and dialogue. Sharp variances of opinion reflected both the differing experiences of churches and theological divergences; and the workshop report did not so much resolve the differences as acknowledge them.

Because of the particular contexts of those who took part most intensively in the dialogue discussions at the meeting, relations between Muslims and Christians had the most prominence. WCC Dialogue Sub-unit director Wesley Ariarajah warned against the oversimplified and sometimes hysterical talk among Christians about the existence of an "Islamic conspiracy", financed by oil money, to wipe out Christianity. But it was clear that in several countries where Islam has shown a militant face, sometimes with the support of the government, churches live in what one group called a "paralysis of fear".

"In view of the highly aggressive, resurgent and militant or politicized contemporary movements among other faiths," Workshop II report said, "we deplore the prejudices, lop-sided views, misunderstandings, questionable methods to the extent of the use of violence, not only by members of any one particular faith but of all, including so-called Christian nations who perpetrate the same sin in subtler manners."

Interfaith dialogue is not just a matter of intellectual conversations in which persons of diverse convictions compare their religious beliefs, but is relevant to issues of justice, peace and the survival of human community. As Michael McCormack of Guyana noted, the most important dialogue is often that which emerges naturally from the experience of working together with other religious groups in a struggle for human rights or against poverty. And a European participant said churches should be challenged to ask themselves how they can even consider "dialogue" with members of another faith when their attitudes towards the adherents of that faith are so often tinged with racism.

Relationships with what are called New Religious Movements is an emerging issue for churches and ecumenical bodies in many places. These NRMs vary greatly among each other — and there is no agreed list of what groups should be included under this rubric. Some NRMs have discernibly Christian origins; and NCC relationships with them are similar to their relationships with "para-church" groups. Others are outgrowths of Eastern religions or philosophies, and the question of relating to them is similar to that of relating to people of other faiths. The workshop report suggested that dialogue with adherents of NRMs is possible only if it is undertaken ecumenically. Three issues were accented: (1) the claims of these movements to offer a new source of spirituality; (2) religious freedom; (3) pastoral concern for those involved with NRMs.

5. Relations with government

Relationships of NCCs to their governments range widely from country to country, across a spectrum whose two poles are marked by what a workshop report called "unanswered questions": How does a state church witness? How does a church witness where the government sees *any* criticism as disloyalty?

There was not much discussion of *whether* NCCs should be "involved in politics"; in general, it was recognized that their very existence — again, with differences from place to place — is a political reality. And, as someone suggested, those church people who argue loudest that the church should steer clear of politics will be crowding the lobbies of the legislature and pulling every string they can put their fingers on if a law is proposed or promulgated that threatens the wealth and power of their church.

As one small group put it, NCCs are essential as "umbrellas and voices of the churches on issues and problems that a single church cannot face in isolation, including encounters with international bodies and governments".

If NCCs do not demonstrate concern about the plight of all the people in their society, they will have no credibility. That means, as Beyers Naudé put it, that they cannot opt out of the struggle. If we profess to have taken an "option for the poor", he said, then it follows that we are unsatisfied with our present society. That is not to say that it will be easy to follow through with this option for the poor on a national level.

Cautionary notes were expressed — questions about the extent of the church's competence to address political issues. Or, to put it in terms of a question raised by one workshop report: how can we really tell whether our government is behaving justly or unjustly? The rule of thumb suggested — "To what extent does the government permit or promote the right of some to live at the expense of others?" — may sometimes help to answer that question. But it is clear, as Jean Skuse of the Australian Council of Churches said, that churches and ecumenical bodies must engage in careful and continuing analysis of social issues.

One of the small group reports judged that "it is progressively becoming necessary for churches to defy states in order to survive". Needless to say, such an adversary relationship may elicit considerable hostility from the government. In the workshop on the "social and political context of councils", there was considerable exchange of opinion about how an NCC should react when its programmes, its leadership or its very existence are targeted for attack. Even when the attacks are without foundation and the threats do not materialize, Jean Skuse noted, the NCC may expend so much time and energy on defending itself that it can't get its work done.

Various suggestions were made for dealing with opposition (which has sometimes included death threats against ecumenical leaders); but few hard and fast rules emerged. Sometimes publicizing a threat may be sufficient for defusing it. But, as WCC international affairs staff member Erich Weingärtner put it: "There *are* death squads out there in some places. And if being attacked by the media should sometimes be seen as a badge of honour, there are also times when that kind of bad publicity can destroy a council."

Relationships between national councils and the government are not necessarily hostile. In some countries churches may view the social order as an instrument that can in fact help a divided Christian community to come to a better understanding of each other as they cooperate for the common good of the whole society rather than endlessly competing with each other.

In many cases national councils of churches receive money from governments to carry out their programmes. Reporting on what he called a "full" workshop discussion of this question, Kenyon Wright said that "some felt there are circumstances in which accepting government funds could compromise a Council's policies. But the group as a whole did not feel we could make a general pronouncement about it." And so the workshop report left the question unanswered.

6. International relations

The relationships of a national council of churches do not stop at the country's frontiers, although international links often go undeveloped simply because the council, weak in resources, is overwhelmed by the magnitude of the task of acting as an agent of unification and reconciliation in its own national situation.

At the Geneva meeting the issue of an NCC's international ecumenical relationships was first broached in the opening panel discussion. Representatives of three different types of ecumenical organization — the WCC, regional ecumenical organizations (REOs) and NCCs — sought to arrive at some clarity on the vocation of NCCs within the one ecumenical movement.

Wesley Ariarajah began his presentation with a simple anecdote illustrating the most common misunderstanding of the relationship between ecumenical organizations at the global, regional and national levels. An aspirant for a WCC scholarship, he said, had written in a letter to the WCC: "I understand that I should begin by applying to the national council of churches, *your branch here in Sri Lanka.*"

What that reflects, said Ariarajah, is a notion of ecumenical relationships structured in a sort of hierarchy, with the largest body being the most powerful and the smaller bodies respectively subsumed under it. If that model were correct, however, the WCC should be made up of regional ecumenical organizations, which should in turn be constituted of NCCs. In fact, the councils at all three "levels" are fellowships of *churches*, which often will belong to the national, regional and world councils all at the same time.

Where structure takes primacy over fellowship, Ariarajah said, the NCC can easily be reduced to a local post office box number for the WCC, the WCC can become an alibi for ecumenical neglect at the local level and the venerable ecumenical insight that unity must be expressed locally "in each place and in all places" is lost.

But if hierarchy isn't the correct way to understand the relationships between the NCC and the REO in its region and between the NCC and the WCC, how should they be seen?

There seemed to be little disagreement in theory about the sort of mutuality that ought to characterize the relationship between the WCC as fellowship of churches and the NCC as fellowship of churches. One participant suggested that "the WCC is the best *sign* we have of the global universal church. Its task is to enable and to equip." Ideally, the WCC is uniquely placed to gather and share, analyze and articulate perspectives that are beyond the horizon of any individual national situation.

But this vision is at best only partly realized. Headquartered in prosperous and neutral Switzerland, the WCC may be insulated from the realities of the daily struggles and crises facing NCCs. At the same time, what the WCC is and does is often little known at the national and local levels. Sometimes that may be deliberate: a report from one small group cited a participant's remark that ecumenism in his country was seen almost entirely as a local phenomenon, partly to avoid what are seen as controversial ideas introduced by the WCC. More often, perhaps, it is a failure of communication. A number of participants, themselves at some remove from the "grassroots", conceded that they were ignorant of much of what is going on at the global ecumenical level through the WCC.

The WCC invests a lot of resources in studies, it was noted, but it seems as if the same questions keep coming up. Do people know what the WCC is doing — or how it works? An African participant suggested that, except for a few areas — aid, refugee service and development — the WCC is too far removed from the local scene on his continent.

A church leader from the Caribbean suggested that relationships might be richer if more resources were devoted to training. Rupert Young of Jamaica added that "gathering up the suffering of local churches" to see what a global emphasis can do might strengthen ties between the NCCs and the WCC. From several sources the suggestion was made that the WCC should assign a full-time staff member to the issue of relationships with NCCs.

Complicating the question of NCCs' international ecumenical relationships is the presence of another level of ecumenical bodies — the REOs. Noting that no matter how the relationships are described, the REOs always seem to be in the middle, Sang Jung Park said the essence of regionalization was the "affirmation of the pluralistic realities of the ecumenical movement" and attestation of the need for "a creative tension between the institutionalized expression of the ecumenical movement and the varied living ecumenical initiatives of the people". Park suggested that regionalization has helped to move the ecumenical agenda away from an excessive focus on European issues.

Ariarajah called for mutual accountability between REOs and the WCC, using as an example the WCC's call to the churches to engage in a process of mutual commitment for justice, peace and the integrity of creation. "There is no way that JPIC can be built here in Geneva and pushed out to the regions. At the same time, there is no way the regions can understand the magnitude of the problems of injustice, militarism and war and environmental destruction without learning about the global connections among these issues."

The relations between the WCC and the REOs were to be taken up in greater detail at an April 1987 meeting in Geneva. But how do NCCs relate to REOs? Michael McCormack warned the WCC against substituting REOs for NCCs in the ecumenical debate. Keeping in contact with 90 NCCs, he conceded, is much more untidy and time-consuming than keeping in touch with seven REOs (plus the two NCCs in countries where there is no REO — Canada and the US). But he suggested that the need for a systematic input from the NCCs into the international ecumenical agenda outweighs the inconvenience of soliciting that input.

7. Relating to each other

A final category of relationships is that typified by the Geneva meeting: relationships between and among NCCs themselves.

What numerous small group reports said in a variety of ways was summed up in the report of Workshop V: "We must be able to share more fully and regularly each other's experiences." But despite this enthusiasm for increased contacts between representatives of NCCs around the world and general agreement about their value, there was not a great deal of clarity or explicitness about how to achieve them.

Sharing of similar experiences may be helpful, but some participants also highlighted the value of sharing from different contexts and perspectives. One participant, for example, expressed gratitude for the insights in Hervé Legrand's paper, observing that she found it especially valuable since the council of churches she represented was not at that level of theological understanding. One small group report proposed that contacts between councils which take major initiatives on social justice and peace issues and those which do not might foster a helpful process of mutual learning.

Besides learning together, contacts between NCCs can serve to build solidarity with those living through particular difficulties. A representative from a third-world country emphasized the importance of "South-South" messages of solidarity in his context: "Our government can too easily ignore or dismiss messages of solidarity that come from European or North American councils of churches," he said. "They would find it much harder to write off a message of support coming, say, from churches in Africa."

At the same time, he challenged NCCs in the South not to ignore the value of their expressing solidarity with councils of churches in the North. "We're so often preoccupied with our own problems, which seem so large, that we don't take time to think about anyone else's problems or consider that we might have something to share with them."

Jean Skuse suggested that one practical step forward might be to use NCCs as a direct channel to take things up with the foreign affairs ministry in their country.

Almost universal was the suggestion that a third global consultation of NCCs should take place in fewer than 15 years. But there was no consensus on when or where it ought to be or what its agenda should be.

III. Challenges for the future

If the variety of relationships that national councils must cope with, develop and balance provides a useful peg on which to hang many of the

discussions that took place during the Geneva meeting, there is nevertheless a risk in paying too much attention to relationships. Scanning the
group and workshop reports, discussions and recommendations from the
meeting in an attempt to identify some of the challenges facing NCCs in
the closing years of the twentieth century points to issues that seem to
merit a higher priority than "relationship-building".

In his opening sermon, Allan Kirton set the danger of focusing on
relationships in sharp relief: "Can it be that we are guilty of skimming the
surface, of being preoccupied with the wrong things? The level of
ecumenical politeness is such that no one wants to say or do anything that
could possibly cause offence. Consequently, nothing that really matters,
that involves risk, is undertaken."

Later that was echoed by a church leader from elsewhere in the
Caribbean, who described the NCC in his country as "a polite club"
which has never managed to galvanize pulpit or pew except once, briefly,
when the issue of a code of ethics for elections was on the national
agenda.

What are some of the major issues that NCCs will have to face in the
years ahead? Different observers of the Geneva meeting and of the
ecumenical scene might mention challenges other than those listed below
or place the accents on different elements. And the four challenges
outlined here include some overlapping: (1) strengthening the instruments
for ecumenism within a country; (2) moving (often against considerable
resistance) to greater communion among the churches; (3) overcoming
the corrosive effects that attach inevitably to any NCC involvement in
receiving and distributing material resources from outside; and (4) identifying models for genuinely ecumenical learning.

Cutting across all of these are the ecclesiological issues that some
would identify as the crux of the contemporary ecumenical challenge.

1. Strengthening national ecumenism

How can existing NCCs be strengthened? What can be done to create
NCCs where there are none?

At one level, this can be seen as a question of structures. And if
"ecclesiological" questions make people nervous or irritated, "structural"
questions are likely to leave them yawning.

The SPCU document on local ecumenism observes that "what really
matters is not the creation of new structures, but the collaboration of
Christians in prayer, reflection and action, based on common baptism and
on a faith which on many essential points is also common". Still, as the

report of one of the small groups at the Geneva meeting emphasized, Christians must be aware of and open to "the presence and leading of the Holy Spirit *in the institutions and structures* of the church".

In fact, another "building" image used at the meeting in connection with national councils has even more profound implications than "structure". Kjell-Ove Nilsson of the Nordic Ecumenical Council said that in the New Testament the word "church" is used either for the local body of believers or for the universal church. Are we prepared, he wondered, to look at national churches (and thus also at NCCs) as a necessary evil — a sort of scaffolding to be taken away once the building is constructed?

The word "structure" evokes images of inflexibility and immobility rather than freedom and adaptability. It hardly suggests acknowledgment of the insight of one small group who said that NCCs have to move beyond the status quo, not become part of it.

Jose Ivo Lorscheiter of Brazil warned that responsiveness to the diversity of challenges facing NCCs makes it necessary to avoid structures that are too rigid. Michael Adhikari, speaking out of his experience in Bangladesh, where 99 percent of the people are Muslims and the 280,000 Christians are in thirty different denominations, observed that "Christianity is an expensive religion because it is a structural religion. Muslims and Hindus, by contrast, have a *community* discipline."

National councils around the world have evolved a variety of structures, more often, perhaps, in response to aspects of their situation — expectations of member churches, sources and limitations of funds, relations to society as a whole — than to a carefully worked out scheme of what the structure of an NCC ought to be.

In a number of countries, ecumenical agencies for aid or mission complicate the total structural problem for the NCC. This is perhaps especially true where there are relief agencies that receive and channel large sums of aid and development money.

Sr Joan Delaney of the WCC staff observed that one challenge in thinking about ways to strengthen NCCs and other ecumenical bodies is the absence of a distinctive style of Christian organization — and the resulting prevalence of what she called a "Western business model".

Some have found a substitute for voting — and the accompanying threats of tyranny by the majority and politicization of church decision-making — in a consensus style of operation: acting and speaking when everyone agrees on what to do or say, remaining silent or inactive otherwise, all the while working to maximize the number of voices heard in forging the consensus. The evident disadvantage of this style is that acting or speaking is perhaps most necessary when there are situations of tension and controversy, so that a council may be immobilized by a failure to achieve consensus precisely when saying or doing something is most crucial.

But if people disagree about structures, no one doubts that the best structure in the world requires able people to make it work effectively. And this was another accent at the meeting: ecumenical leadership for NCCs seems constantly to be in short supply, and in many cases the means to train future leaders are not available.

Sr Joan Delaney remarked on the sheer volume of factual knowledge needed to operate effectively in the ecumenical movement. For example, how many people are more than dimly aware of the origins of schisms and the history of initiatives for church union? Yet these are important for understanding the current situation. Many of the divisions the ecumenical movement seeks to overcome are rooted in different notions of church governance. But most people are only vaguely familiar with their own church order, let alone anyone else's. Where are the resources and the programmes to teach this sort of background material essential to effective ecumenical engagement?

David Bleakley added the unhappy reminder that, because of limited financial resources, those who need training the most are the least likely to get it. And Lal Rinmawia of India pointed out that besides preparing young people for future ecumenical leadership roles, NCCs must persuade the churches to send their best people forward to serve in ecumenical bodies.

A representative from the Solomon Islands said the problem in his area was aggravated by the reluctance of church leaders to get together. Locally, he said, people trust each other and are eager to act ecumenically. But heads of churches seem to fear that ecumenical activities, especially if they are successful, will threaten bilateral support from overseas.

At the end of the day, however, said David Gill, relationships and structures — no matter how important — are not the heart of the issue for NCCs. The crying need is the development of an ecumenical *vision*.

In short, where are we going? At the present time, Gill said, there is a plurality of sometimes conflicting ecumenical visions — in part because of the growth of the ecumenical movement in the last four decades, in part because of what he described as contemporary theological confusion. For a new vision to emerge, Wesley Ariarajah suggested, what is needed is obedience, solidarity and ecumenical discipline.

But for some NCCs, both nuts-and-bolts talk about structures and more elevated discussion of relationships and vision give way to a more pressing concern: survival. As John Kamau of the NCC in Kenya said, many councils live in a "permanent crisis situation", in which survival takes priority over everything else, including leadership development and broadening the vision.

2. Moving towards unity in community

Just how important is church unity in the panoply of things that a national council does or tries to do? There is some indication that the answer depends on "ecumenical geography" — with churches from the "North" and the "South" taking divergent positions. A participant from the Pacific put it sharply; it was his observation, he said, that the people who speak the most about church unity are also the ones who speak the most about structures and size and power.

But it is by no means only in the "third world" that a deliberate preoccupation with visible church unity takes a back seat to what seem more pressing issues. Jocelyn Armstrong said that in New Zealand, where the churches have gone through a long process of forging a new ecumenical instrument to replace the national council of churches, both biculturalism and the community of women and men take priority over the "unity issue" as such. Earlier, in the 1970s, when church union schemes were prominent on New Zealand's ecumenical agenda, this went on quite apart from the national council of churches, which was perceived as "doing social justice".

British Council of Churches general secretary Philip Morgan remarked that the BCC has sometimes not been taken seriously by some Roman Catholic leaders in the country precisely because it did not get involved in church union negotiations — even if the SPCU document makes it clear that this is not the business of a council (except insofar as they are asked by the churches involved to provide administrative assistance).

One small group report phrased what seemed to be a general consensus: national councils should only aim at church *unity* — mutual trust and respect — and leave church *union* to the churches. But there were also several reminders of what had already been said fifteen years ago about national councils becoming an ecumenical "alibi", an excuse for the churches themselves not to move forward on the road to unity. What is gained, it was asked, if churches collaborate on selected issues within the framework of the NCC and all the denominational structures remain in place, unchanged and unchallenged? And how scandalous that representatives from two churches in the same country may encounter each other only in the framework of the WCC, while remaining isolated from each other at home!

And so others put the case for the NCC role in church unity more strongly, saying that national councils should be *intentional* about unity. One group report went so far as to suggest that NCCs ought to *ensure* that theological dialogue takes place at the national level.

There were also expressions of the need for councils to *exemplify* unity. Councils, said the report of Workshop I, are instruments and signs of unity. Much of this talk was in organic terms: councils should be a place where unity grows and develops; it is the vocation of NCCs to foster a fellowship or koinonia of worship among the churches.

A number of people suggested that the split between concern for unity and concern for action in society — the "Faith and Order vs Life and Work" dichotomy which has been with the ecumenical movement from the beginning — is not only artificial but indeed works against both unity and engagement in society. As a small group report said, "how can churches which are divided take a credible stance on issues of justice and peace?"

3. The perils of channelling funds

Does the development tail wag the ecumenical dog? That image, used more than once during the week, points to a crucial challenge for NCCs. To put it less colourfully, when a large part of an NCC's work centres on the transfer of material resources from outside the country, what happens to its own identity? David Gill put the answer bluntly: "Churches come to see ecumenism as a process of receiving money from overseas, and the ecumenical movement loses force as a movement for renewal."

Probably this issue poses the greatest challenge for national councils in developing countries. When the group divided into "workshops" on the major discussion topics identified before the meeting, all of those in the workshop on "finance, service, development and resource sharing" were from NCCs in developing countries. But Philip Morgan pointed out that there is a corrupting factor to the flow of money through ecumenical agencies in "donor" countries as well. What happens? While we talk about "powerlessness", we're forced to deal with power.

The deleterious things that can happen when processing money takes up most of an NCC's time and energy are familiar enough. Misappropriation of funds is probably the least of the threats. Far more serious are such long-term consequences as the imposition of "alienating structures" from outside (the national council has to organize its activities along lines imported from elsewhere), the ignoring of other essential services that national councils ought to be providing to their member churches, the exacerbation of existing tensions (channelling money to some people or groups of course channels it away from others), and perhaps worst of all the development of dependency in the "receiving" country. Dependency has not only to do with neglect of local resources in favour of the quick fix from an infusion of outside material aid. It also erodes self-reliance, so that the ability to make effective decisions is stunted and poverty is perpetuated.

Despite such baleful consequences — none of them imaginary or theoretical — the workshop report remained open to the possibility that NCCs, as a manifestation of unity, might have as one of their roles the channelling of funds from others in the ecumenical family, other agencies, even government.

At the same time there was an insistence that channelling money should only be seen as a temporary expedient, though the workshop report acknowledged just how many obstacles stand in the way of self-sufficiency for churches in most parts of the developing world: the international economic situation, the limited funds available to local churches and the lack of management expertise to operate long-term income-generating projects.

4. Models of learning

A final challenge for NCCs is that of ecumenical learning — specifically, how to learn from each other.

A list (in the Workshop II report) of "reasons for having NCCs" was based in part on stories of positive experiences of different types of collaboration among churches in many different countries heard at the meeting. Some of these closely involved an NCC; in other cases, things seemed to work well without particular support from the national council.

But how do accounts of what has been effective in one situation get translated into implications for policy for NCCs elsewhere? This question was one of the preoccupations of Workshop V, which discussed social and political involvements of NCCs.

To be sure, solidarity is in itself important. There is a value — even a need — to tell and hear stories from each other, the workshop said. But beyond solidarity comes a clear call for common understandings of what we do and why — both from a biblical and theological perspective and from the point of view of social and political analysis. Besides positive models and visions of exercises in collaboration among churches, we should develop positive models and visions of the alternative society we are seeking. But that, of course, opens up new risks of disagreement and fragmentation as well.

One idea raised was that of *ad hoc* "networking" of two or more councils for a limited period of time to confront a specific issue that affects all of them. Some recent examples of this were cited — in particular, cooperation between churches in Japan and Korea over the treatment of foreigners (especially Koreans) in Japan. Also in the last several years, at the regional level, the Christian Conference of Asia and the Middle East Council of Churches have worked together on the problems facing migrant workers in the Gulf States, many of whom come from Asia; and the WCC, in cooperation with REOs, organized a human rights exposure and reflection programme for church leaders from Asia and Latin America.

* * *

How are the long-term effects of the Geneva meeting to be evaluated? Certainly the opportunity to reaffirm old friendships and develop new ones is not unimportant for the common struggle. Even if ecumenists cannot expect the dramatic reversal of fortunes that Simon Peter enjoyed when he did as Jesus said and cast his net into the deep once more, the discouragement about which Allan Kirton spoke in his opening sermon is less likely to persist when they can be strengthened by solidarity with others facing similar struggles and problems.

Beyers Naudé observed that it would be impossible for the SACC to respond meaningfully in its situation without the constant fellowship, debate, discussion, concern expressed by Christians elsewhere. "I hope and pray", he said, "that the day will come when we will be able to return in gratitude to you what you have been giving to us. But it is also true that out of our struggle a witness is being presented to councils around the world of how we understand God's will for a people in pain and suffering, struggling to obtain liberation and a church renewed and revitalized in its witness to the world."

If the "pep talk" function was an important dimension of the meeting, what of the documents that emerged from the five workshops? For the most part these sought to summarize the discussions that took place rather than to forge new consensus statements, articulate theological insights with new precision or make concrete and measurable practical recommendations. Since the documents were understood not to be authoritative, there was perhaps a tendency to include most of what was said in the discussions, rather than to rank it according to what was crucial, what was important, what was interesting and what would probably turn out to be impractical.

Some may wonder, finally, how much importance the meeting really had for those outside of the small circle of professional ecumenists. In its details, perhaps not very much. But at a deeper level, the question of the importance of this meeting is really the question of how important it is to work for unity "in each place and in all places" — and ultimately of how important the ecumenical movement itself is. For those who take seriously the prayer of Jesus "that all may be one", the answer seems clear... "so that the world might believe".

The Life and Meaning of NCCs:
the Ecclesiological Issues

THOMAS F. BEST

National councils of churches (NCCs) are one of the most widespread, prominent and important expressions of the ecumenical movement, and their second world consultation, held 20-24 October 1986, was long overdue. Since the last such gathering, in 1971, dramatic changes have taken place in the churches, the ecumenical movement, and the world in which we live. The purpose of the consultation was both general and vital: to enable the NCCs to share their visions, perspectives and experiences, their successes, failures, problems and opportunities — in short, to enable their mutual enrichment and empowerment, and to bring their witness and wisdom into the ecumenical movement as a whole.

An important by-product of the meeting was the "reception" of, and reflection on, the continuing discussion of the ecclesiological significance of NCCs. Very significant developments have occurred in this area since the 1971 NCCs meeting, and this more than anything else had led to the call for the consultation in 1986. [1]

Here we shall give an overview of some important developments since the previous NCCs consultation, survey the progress of the ecclesiological discussion, focusing on the fundamental and persisting issues, and then suggest a specific task for NCCs in the future.

Developments since 1971

A fundamental task of the NCCs at their meeting in 1971 was to identify — and, in a sense, to justify — their role in relation to their own member churches. Victor Hayward, then WCC secretary for relationships with national and regional councils, found that this "very seldom appears satisfactory... A council committee usually means a gathering of church leaders to decide what the council shall do, instead of what their churches should do together through the council."[2] Councils felt their own position to be ambiguous, if not schizophrenic: on the one hand, "councils are created by the churches to serve, and this role is happily accepted"; but sometimes "... councils are required to give leadership on particular issues, and to pioneer boldly into areas where churches fear to tread alone".[3] And this was symptomatic of a more fundamental problem:

> The difficulty most common to our councils is that some churches have self-contradictory attitudes towards us. On the one hand, churches believe they should pass over to councils only a very small fraction of their work and a strictly limited mandate. On the other hand, those same churches expect more service from the council than it is possible to give.[4]

Additional problems were identified in an address to the consultation in which Lukas Vischer, then director of Faith and Order, noted three "impasses" in which the NCCs found themselves. The first was that they did not include "as far as possible *all* churches and Christians who are engaged in the ecumenical movement in a specific area".[5] At this point Vischer had in mind particularly the absence of the Roman Catholic Church from most NCCs. This not only meant that the NCCs and the Roman Catholic Church were deprived of essential ecumenical contacts. It also led — since some cooperation was inevitable, particularly in the practical field — to a proliferation of ad hoc structures outside the NCCs, thus scattering precious ecumenical time and energy.[6]

The second area of concern was the absence of reflection in most NCCs on "faith and order" issues, i.e. on the differences in theology and practice which separate their member churches:

> ...on the whole, Christian councils have left the divisions between the churches intact. Generally speaking, they have been an agency for carrying out certain joint tasks rather than an instrument of unity... The result is that... they have become a structure alongside the churches, with its own momentum... All questions relating to unity have been expressly reserved by the constitution of the council to the churches themselves. The council is to deal exclusively with external matters which raise no awkward questions about the character, order and self-understanding of the individual churches themselves.[7]

> But the very existence of councils implies the need for theological work towards unity. The churches themselves recognize that their division is sin against the one body of Christ, and, as Vischer put it, "Christian councils are the structural expression of this shared conviction, this common commitment... The Christian councils are, so to speak, the thorn in the flesh of the

churches. They are a constant reminder to the churches of the anomalous situation [of division] in which they live."[8]

Vischer's third and most important issue was the relation of Christian councils to the manifold movements and unofficial groups which had sprung up to give a Christian witness on particular issues of peace and justice. These often stood in an uneasy relationship to the very churches which had, in many cases, spawned them, but Vischer insisted that "movements and groups must be able to feel themselves to be an integral part of the Christian councils...".[9] The point was taken by the 1971 consultation, which challenged councils to be a place for dialogue between such "movements" and the churches, so that both could benefit: "They often represent a valid challenge to the slowness of the churches... on the other hand, the impetus they provide runs the risk of being dissipated... unless it is somehow related to ongoing structures."[10]

Even a brief survey reveals considerable progress since 1971 in the first two of these "impasses". The membership of NCCs has steadily broadened, due especially to the dramatic increase of Roman Catholic participation — from full membership in 11 councils reported in 1971[11] to 19 in 1975[12] to 33 in 1982,[13] not to mention the many places where Roman Catholics are present as observers or cooperate in specific areas of a council's work. Orthodox participation continues to be a regular and valuable aspect of the life of NCCs. With some important exceptions pentecostal and evangelical Protestants are not actively involved, and sometimes even have "umbrella" organizations of their own. On the other hand, in some places where NCC membership is not yet possible, various churches have joined in looser, but still very significant, associations (for example the Christian Federation of Malaysia, which links the members of the Christian Council of Malaysia with the Roman Catholic Church and with evangelical Protestants).

There has been a significant advance in the councils' work towards Christian unity, to the point where many councils now regard theological discussion of divisions among their member churches as an inescapable part of their mandate. Several factors have contributed to this. The conviction has grown within the ecumenical movement as a whole that the old dichotomy between unity and mission, between "faith and order" issues and "witness and service" issues, is false and destructive. Here *Baptism, Eucharist and Ministry* has offered an important lead in its insistence that both baptism and eucharist point inevitably to Christian work for justice and reconciliation in a divided and hurting world. [14] There is a stronger sense that Christian action must proceed from biblical and theological reflection and, from the Faith and Order perspective, a new awareness that "divisions" include not only abstract, technical theological problems but also the symptoms of the brokenness of the human community: the churches are divided not only from each other over the doctrine of transubstantiation but also, and perhaps more persistently and destructively, within themselves by racism, discrimination due to sex or social status, and other factors.

Finally, the broadening of council membership, particularly where the Roman Catholic Church has been involved, has led to renewed reflection upon the role of the Council and its relation to its member churches. This we will treat in more detail later on.

In short, many would now agree with the statement of Cardinal Willebrands: "... if a council is content to be only a service and development agency, if it does not have a conscious thrust forward in the cause of ecclesial unity... then it is simply failing to exercise its potential". [15] Yet this ecumenical conviction must still be "received" at the local level; there remain councils fully absorbed in cooperative action, with no time or energy left for reflection on the theological and ecclesiological grounds for their action, much less their mandate for unity. And in some cases local church leaders are unaware of, or even resist for various reasons, the impulses towards unity which their own confessions have already embraced. [16]

Vischer's third concern, the relation of the NCCs to action movements and unofficial groups, remains the most problematic. It is noteworthy that many of the social concerns current in 1971 have been taken up by councils and by their member churches. Insofar as we can speak of such an "institutionalization of the prophetic", it is a victory for the movements and their witness. Yet the most progressive of the movements today are no closer to councils than before, often from their own choice. One fruitful relationship between council and movements has been in Canada, where the Canadian Council of Churches has worked on a whole range of issues not so much through formal council structures as in coalitions with various movements and groups.

To conclude this brief survey, one very important development has been the re-thinking and re-formation of several NCCs, often for the express purpose of including more, and more diverse, churches within them. [17] Such reorganizations may, of course, create problems as well as solve them. The newly-incorporated churches may be much more sensitive in particular areas, for example the question of public statements issued by councils. And when movements and unofficial groups are brought into a more formal structure they are bound to feel burdened by an increase of "bureaucratization".

Perhaps the most creative approach to the creation of a new national ecumenical body has been in New Zealand, where the goal was not only the inclusion of new partners (notably the Roman Catholic Church), but a strong commitment to including the whole people of God (lay and ordained, women and men, young and old) and the adoption of new and more participatory styles of decision-making, along with decentralized administration of the council itself. This is a most significant and promising vision, and its successes and problems will have much to teach the NCCs as a whole.[18]

The ecclesiological significance of NCCs: the developing issues

What has been the basic understanding of the ecclesiological significance of NCCs, and how has this advanced since their first world consultation in 1971? Although the WCC is in some respects a unique case, most churches have understood their membership in NCCs much along the lines of the WCC "Toronto Statement" of 1950. This indicated that membership in the WCC *"does not imply that a Church treats its own conception of the Church as merely relative"*,[19] nor *"the acceptance of a specific doctrine concerning the nature of Church and unity"*,[20] nor again *"... that each Church must regard the other member Churches as Churches in the true and full sense of the word"*.[21] The genius of these negative statements was to enable churches to share reflection and action, to build trust and commitment among themselves, without having first to resolve all the theological, ecclesiological, psychological, logistical and practical(!) factors which divide them.

The positive statements made at Toronto have attracted less attention, but are no less important in visioning the role of a council of churches. Most fundamentally it was affirmed that *"the member Churches of the World Council recognize in other Churches elements of the true Church"*,[22] and that they admit *"that the membership of the Church of Christ is more inclusive than the membership of their own Church body. They seek, therefore, to enter into living contact with those outside their own ranks who confess the Lordship of Christ."*[23] Such a community of churches may enable them both to *grow* together and to grow *together:*

...the life of the Church, as it expresses itself in its witness to its own members and to the world, needs constant renewal. The churches can and should help each other in this realm by a mutual exchange of thought and of experience... There is no intention to impose any particular pattern of thought or life upon the churches. But whatever insight has been received by one or more churches is to be made available to all the churches...[24]

Recently the ecclesiological significance of NCCs has been the subject of intense discussion within the ecumenical movement. Although this was not a primary focus of the 1971 world consultation of NCCs, that meeting did develop two ideas basic to the whole subsequent discussion. The first was the insistence that theological work towards unity was, indeed, basic to the life of NCCs, that "... such matters, which are fundamental to the whole ecumenical movement, be discussed as the real basis for their common witness and action".[25] Second was the idea that the councils, which lack an independent ecclesiological status, are nonetheless "servants" or "instruments" enabling crucial ecclesiological developments to occur among their member churches:

Indeed even now, when churches share in some common life, and witness and act together, a new ecclesial reality appears — not in the council as an organization, but among the member churches as they share this ecumenical experience, through the council's instrumentality.[26]

The ecclesiological discussion has been greatly stimulated and enriched by the entry of Roman Catholic Churches into NCCs, primarily, I think, due to two features of this church. The first is its unique combination of world and local dimensions, which means that Roman Catholic membership in a national council immediately raises — far more than is the case with most of its Protestant counterparts, and in quite a different way from the Orthodox — profound issues of an NCC member church's authority and accountability to a larger confessional body beyond the national level.[27] Second, the Roman Catholic Church does claim — however sympathetically and sensitively nuanced this may be, and with whatever allowances for institutional shortcomings — that its expression of Christianity has a certain definitive or normative character.[28] As a basic Roman Catholic text on ecumenical cooperation states, "... this qualifies significantly the Catholic participation in the ecumenical movement",[29] and must inevitably raise the question of the inter-relationship and equality of the member churches within an NCC. The discussion of these issues — which often have not been faced directly until this point in the life of an NCC — benefits *all* its member churches.

The basic principles of Roman Catholic involvement in NCCs are lucidly explained in the text on ecumenical collaboration just cited. Such involvement is a deeply serious step for the church, as it implies "recognition of other member churches as ecclesial communities",[30] though — by explicit analogy with the WCC Toronto statement — not thereby "diminish[ing] its faith about its uniqueness".[31]

The limitations of councils as seen from the Roman Catholic perspective are carefully and sensitively drawn. Councils "... do not in and of themselves contain in embryo the beginnings of a new Church... They do not claim to be churches nor do they claim authority to commission a ministry of word and sacrament."[32] While Faith and Order questions are essential within its life, a council must not presume to initiate "formal doctrinal conversations between churches", this being the prerogative of the churches themselves in their "immediate and bilateral contacts".[33] Procedures for councils to make public statements must be carefully defined and respectful of the right of each member church to define its own position.[34] And it is essential to have clear lines of accountability from the structures of the various churches to their representatives in the council, who "... while representing the Church on matters within their competence... should be clearly aware of the limits beyond which they cannot commit the Church without prior reference to higher authority".[35]

Within these guidelines there is a strong and clear appeal for the fullest possible involvement of local Roman Catholic churches in NCCs, an appeal which, as we have seen, has borne fruit in the lives of many Councils around the world.

The next major step in the discussion was the "Consultation on the Significance and Contribution of Councils of Churches in the Ecumenical Movement" held in Venice in 1982 under the auspices of the WCC Faith and Order Commission and the Secretariat for Promoting Christian Unity of the Roman Catholic Church. Here the Roman Catholic position received a very creative and forward-looking interpretation by J.M.R. Tillard, O.P., who noted that: "Hitherto ecclesiology ... knows only two states of the Church of God: the state of communion in organic unity and the state of separation or schism";[36] what must be investigated is the ecclesiological status of "interim expressions of unity", present partial realizations of unity by churches committed to each other and to their search for a common future.

The key to Tillard's reflections is his concept of "recognition" among the member churches of a council, resting "... fundamentally on the certainty that the Church of God is present in the other ecclesial groups, at least where some essential conditions are fulfilled".[37] He asserts that no church "having confessional stability" and "honouring its own tradition" accepts the full ecclesial adequacy of its partners within a council of churches.[38] Nonetheless one recognizes the shortcomings of one's own tradition in its empirical life; and from his own perspective Tillard writes of the Roman Catholic Church:

> If she is convinced, with *Lumen Gentium*, that the Church of God *subsists* in herself with what is objectively necessary to its fullness, she recognizes also that the Church of God exists outside herself, though not with everything that is required for that fullness. To go further, she is aware of the sometimes defective state in which certain fundamental ecclesial values are found in herself. Convinced that she possesses what is required for ecclesial fullness, she does not pretend to possess all of it as perfectly as she should. This awareness of deficiency, once officially contradicted by the ecclesiology of the past, is accepted today in most Catholic circles.[39]

This opens the way for a vision of great power and beauty, a vision of the churches sharing their distinctive gifts for the good of the body of Christ, the churches growing together towards the church which God desires:

> The aim of any genuine council of churches... is precisely to allow the churches and ecclesial communities comprising it to provide each other with the means to grow together towards full ecclesial status, each helping the other to acquire what it lacks. There is thus no question of asking one group to absorb the others by imposing its own patterns... once it is clear what is required for full ecclesial status each tries to bring to the other what it needs and in return hopes to receive what it lacks itself.[40]

Ultimately it is a matter of conversion: "It is not enough to be united; we must at the same time be converted to that which God wishes for his Church."[41] This may demand costly sacrifices from the churches, as they learn together the final shape God wills for the church; this must be worked out in theological reflection upon specific, and necessarily difficult, issues. For example, the churches' work together on the theology of ministry "... implies that some groups agree to modify objectively certain of their emphases, that others take on dimensions of ministry that they have hitherto ignored".[42]

Although councils do not represent a final stage of unity, they do have for Tillard "an important ecclesiological status. They already express a unity *in via*, making possible ecclesial acts in common which belong to the very essence of the Church of God";[43] they express "a *germinal* unity (and for that reason prophetic) [*sic*]",[44] and in their "...communion of mission, witness and prayer the full *koinonia* [of the churches in a truly conciliar state] is seen in profile and forecast".[45]

The Venice meeting marked an important stage in the ecclesiological discussion. The consideration of councils is now set in the context of the churches' commitment to the search for unity: if the councils are "servants", they are servants precisely of this search. The churches have embarked "together on the road to full communion and accept that there is no way back..."[46] Thus

> it appears indispensable to the advance towards unity that churches are able to mark irreversible steps; there are no ways back without the creation of new divisions, without shattering a new emerging community. A clear awareness of this condition considerably strengthens the commitment of churches to the ecumenical movement and to the councils of churches in particular.[47]

The cost of serious involvement in a council is now emphasized:

> A council of churches provides an ecclesial situation in which inherited values and elements of separated churches are tested and discerned and in which there is a real though imperfect experience of the future diversity of full conciliar fellowship (*concile*). Such a council (*conseil*) gives a new direction and impetus to the overall life, unity and mission of the church. Membership... expresses *a commitment to practise some real measure of mutual recognition and reconciliation at every level of church life.*[48]

The authentic experience of a council is one of development and growth towards unity, hence "... the structures of councils will need to remain flexible — dynamic — in order to be able to adapt to the constantly growing mutual recognition and to express it visibly in a more and more adequate manner".[49]

Such statements made an insistence upon the councils' servant role all the more striking and — from the point of view of the sovereignty of the member churches — necessary. Councils, then, "are not the goal of the unity we seek, but a path towards that goal. The experience of unity acquired in the framework of the council does not belong to the council but belongs wholly to the churches which compose the council. The councils... will disappear at the moment of unity."[50]

In addition Venice emphasized two themes which may become central to the ecclesiological discussion of councils in the years ahead. First, it assumed a dynamic interaction between the local and universal levels of the church (and, by the same token, of the individual member churches of an NCC). On the one hand it "... is the assembly of Christians in unity in a given place... which is the starting point for the growth of the church of

God. It is also in the local community, therefore, that the construction of unity or the common growth in unity must be rooted";[51] on the other, "... local initiatives must be brought to the forum of the church as a whole". [52]

Second was a frank and mature admission that some conflicts may arise in the context of NCCs. These can occur at the institutional level, as member churches encounter points of persistent, genuine disagreement over theological issues, or make difficult "strategic" decisions about council programmes. Some degree of conflict is inevitable when significant issues are in play; the question is not whether it will happen, but whether it can be faced in a constructive and instructive way:

> Member churches, as well as councils of churches, have to learn to live with conflicts and to deal with them in such a way that they do not destroy communion. This can prepare them to help the council as it faces similar conflicts and as it promotes structures which may eventually be acceptable for a church which is truly united. [53]

Another type of conflict is the more difficult and poignant in being personalized:

> Commitment to the cause of unity in the framework of a council of churches quite often will lead to a tension between two loyalties: loyalty to an inherited tradition believed to be normative and loyalty to the growing together into unity. This tension has to be accepted and cannot be solved by giving up one of the two loyalties; on the contrary, the churches must learn to live with it, in order to transcend this tension in the Spirit, often in unpredictable ways. [54]

For such tensions are not experienced by "the churches" in the abstract, but by persons who compose the body of Christ, persons whose very Christian and church commitment draws them together to glimpse a vision of unity which sometimes seems more compelling and precious than the divided traditions which have fostered it. And it is precisely those who are most deeply committed who will feel this tension of divided loyalties most deeply.

With this we come to the present second world consultation of national councils of churches. This consolidated and advanced the ecclesiological reflection on councils in several areas. It was striking that the more "issue-oriented" of the two major consultation papers, that by Jean Skuse, began "... with the basic assumption that councils of churches exist primarily to promote the unity God wills for the church... we all have a common goal of unity within the church as a sign of the unity we long for for the whole of humanity..."[55]

The whole paper repays careful reading precisely from the ecclesiological point of view.

In the second, and more explicitly theological, paper Hervé Legrand wrestled creatively with all the major issues in the ecclesiological debate about councils of churches.[56] Here we can only indicate his most significant and salient reflections which came, I believe, in three areas. The first was the status of councils as "instruments" of the churches in their search for unity. For Legrand, the councils as instruments may indeed offer a "foretaste" of the ultimate "conciliar"[57] unity of the church:

> In so far as councils have been able to share their experience with the people of their churches, this will in fact have been a preconciliar experience; it will have made it possible to have a foretaste of what it would be to live in unity in diversity and harmony, confessing the one same faith — the essential characteristics of conciliar life.[58]

But if the councils are instrumental, they are *only* instrumental; Legrand emphasizes that they must not be viewed as a kind of "embryonic church".[59]

Second, Legrand calls attention to the relation between the local and universal "levels" of the church. The competence of NCCs "is, by definition, national"; they "have the primary duty of drawing the attention of all their member churches to their Christian responsibility in the national setting". But he pleads for a realistic awareness of the "legitimate ecclesiological difficulties", within the NCC context, of churches with a worldwide dimension.[60] As we shall see, this is a critical area for further study.

Legrand's third focus is the councils' role in promoting the "reception" of ecumenical dialogues. His suggestions for councils in relation to bilateral dialogues are particularly visionary and creative: over against their member churches involved in bilaterals, councils "can play a very valuable role as a neutral third party". They can "encourage the two partners to be more open and forward-looking in their decisions, to refrain perhaps from taking the easy way out in solving certain questions and, on other points, to set way-marks towards a wider unity".[61] Here, if I understand aright, the councils are invited to draw very near to the churches' autonomous bilateral discussions, in a sense to "claim" them on behalf of the ecumenical movement as a whole, and to offer suggestions and a critique to the specific churches involved.

Finally we come to the most recent work in this area, as represented by Workshop I on ecclesiological issues at the 1986 consultation.[62] This workshop was not intended to produce technical theological results; its purpose was to foster a broader "reception" of the earlier ecclesiological discussion, and to test its results with the leadership of NCCs. Participants included both professional theologians and persons, with varying types of training and experience, who are deeply involved in the leadership of both local churches and NCCs. As often happens in such mixed groups, serious theological reflections did indeed result — which were all the more profound for being rooted in the life of the church at the local level. And the ecclesiological discussion was advanced at several points, of which here we can mention only some of the most significant.

It appears, first, that *koinonia* is emerging as a unifying ecclesiological concept for NCCs — as indeed for other areas of the ecumenical movement.[63] The power of this concept is that koinonia not only "makes possible our unity in diversity",[64] it does so while affirming the value of our diverse elements, and celebrating the creative and sustaining interaction among them. The model is ultimately Trinitarian, as seen in the following statement from Workshop I:

> The Triune God — whose being is koinonia — calls the church to koinonia (communion, fellowship, partnership, community) in confession, worship and life. We believe that this koinonia clarifies the vision of unity which we seek and should be a matter for further theological reflection.[65]

Second, there was a strong reaffirmation that the unity of the church exists not only for its own sake — to the glory of God, who wills that the body of Christ be one — but also, crucially, for the sake of the world which Christ died to save. The unity of the church must be set and seen within the wider unity of humanity, for God created all and desires that all may have fullness of life. This is the theological foundation for our conviction that "the unity of the church and the search for the unity, justice and peace of humanity belong dynamically together".[66]

This was matched, third, by an important methodological conclusion: "... councils of churches are often able to discover a deeper unity when they have looked beyond themselves and have engaged together in common witness and action. But such common action has often required further reflection on fundamental theological issues." This is identified as an "essential dynamic of reflection and action, action and reflection",[67] suggesting a circular hermeneutic which grounds theological reflection in human experience, while exposing that experience to the witness of scripture and tradition.

This approach has proved helpful elsewhere in moving beyond the sterile and artificial division between "theology" and "action".[68]

Fourth, beginning theologically from the idea of koinonia means that *all* the people of God must share, in ways that are appropriate, in the life and witness of the church. The call for increased "participation" in the church is not a fad, but a necessary response to the biblical imperative that all our "gifts" be brought to build up the body of Christ. NCCs, it was affirmed, must set an example and, where required, offer leadership to their own member churches:

> National councils of churches are called to reflect in their patterns of working this imperative towards participation, and to create a context within which their member churches may challenge each other to explore new ways in which such fuller participation may be possible in their *koinonia* of confession, worship and action. We believe this to be an urgent challenge. [69]

And this should lead NCCs and their member churches to a much greater sensitivity in working with groups who have been largely excluded from the life of the church, and in recognizing "cultural patterns" which block participation. [70]

Some persistent issues

Our survey of the ecclesiological discussion reveals an emerging common line of thought — certainly not yet a consensus, but some agreement as to what the issues are and how they might be approached. Several problems seem to be particularly persistent, and are likely to be crucial in the continuing debate.

One such question is the relation between local and universal expressions of the church. Here we must sort out what is, in fact, under discussion. Does the term "universal church" mean the body of Christ in its fullness, that final ecclesial reality towards which the different confessions, in their different ways, orient themselves? Or does it refer to the highest level of authority of a particular confession, of which the national churches of that confession all around the world are parts? When the Venice report says that "local initiatives [towards unity] must be brought to the forum of the Church as a whole", [71] is this an appeal to the Christian tradition "as a whole", to the long history of its faith and witness as a touchstone for all the churches — in the manner of the famous question asked of the churches by *BEM* [72] — or does it, in the end, amount only to a matter of internal discipline within the respective confessions?

It must be clarified whether the Venice report already presupposes a certain understanding of the relation of the different "levels" of the church, that is, a certain understanding of the nature of the church itself.

Perhaps the term "levels", with its spatial metaphor, should be avoided altogether; to the extent that it implies a certain ecclesiological orientation, it confuses rather than clarifies the discussion. At any rate, Hervé Legrand shows an admirable sensitivity to the issue in insisting that discussions towards unity within NCCs "must take place on a footing of equality... the fact that some churches have the structures of a world communion while others are national in scope does not affect this equality". [73]

But the fact remains that we have not probed all the implications of the fundamental distinction between national churches which are, juridically, autonomous; national churches which understand themselves to come, in some sense, within the ethos and authority of a world communion; and national churches which are themselves members of a world church. It may be that clearer and more forceful expression of all the basic ecclesiological options is required before a consensus can be shaped.

A second basic issue is the "purely instrumental" nature of councils of churches. If the issue is as clear as everyone says it is, why does it refuse to go away? The persistence of the issue shows that something is at stake, something sensitive and difficult perhaps not so much theologically or ecclesiologically as psychologically and emotionally. Their insistence that councils are only "instruments" of the churches themselves for their mission and service in the world, and for their search for unity, has helped the churches to encourage the councils in their positive role. It has meant that the councils need not be regarded in any sense as "threats" to their member churches, and has enabled the councils to develop both programmatically and theologically. [74]

And yet the "instrumental" position is easier to maintain in the world of abstract thought than in the reality of everyday life, where Christians engage in common reflection and action, and make their commitments to each other and to institutions and ideals. When persons encounter Christian community (koinonia) through an ecumenical experience in a council of churches, it is difficult to convince them that the ecclesial reality "really" inheres in the divided churches — especially when, as is sadly still sometimes the case, such experiences seem to happen in spite of the churches rather than because of them.

Thus whatever qualifications may be necessary for the "sovereignty" of their member churches, it is essential that the full value of councils be celebrated and stressed. This is the importance of Tillard's insistence that councils can express "a *germinal* unity... which has real ecclesial density", [75] and Legrand's affirmation that councils can have a genuinely "preconciliar" dimension.[76] Here the Venice report is helpful in addressing openly the question of "divided loyalties".[77] In addition it is striking that the 1986 consultation mentioned the theme of councils as not only instruments but "signs" of unity.[78] This could be a promising line of thought, when linked with the concept of the church as sign, and should be taken up in the next stages of the discussion.

As we have seen, the councils have received an astonishing amount of creative ecclesiological attention in the short fifteen years between their first and second world consultations. Such a burst of theological energy is a good "sign"; it means that the churches involved feel touched in important ways, that their self-understanding and, indeed, their exercise of authority, has been addressed — in other words, that significant issues have been raised for the benefit of the churches, the NCCs, and the ecumenical movement as a whole.

A new role for NCCs? A modest proposal

Finally, it is worth asking how the NCCs can best focus their energies today: in the present ecumenical climate, what unifying factor could most creatively link their diverse programmes and reflections? Here it is necessary to recall two factors which have been decisive in the search for unity. One is the WCC Faith and Order text *Baptism, Eucharist and Ministry*, which has been brilliantly successful in engaging the churches in common reflection upon issues of theology and practise which continue to divide them. This "multilateral" approach is complemented, second, by the various international bilateral discussions, which seek to build understanding and to resolve specific historic and theological differences between pairs of churches at the world level. Both approaches have led to genuine breakthroughs in ecumenical understanding and relations.

Both *BEM* and the bilaterals, of course, have worked within the framework of the historic divisions between the churches. These divisions occurred in the context of Europe and the Middle East, and were articulated in the language and thought-forms of classical Western theology; it is inevitable that, for example, both *BEM* and the official responses from the churches should speak this "Western" language. And this has been true even of most "non-Western" responses, those from churches in Latin America, Asia, Africa and the Pacific, due to the patterns of Christian life and thought which have been imposed or inherited from the West and because theological training still follows largely classical, Western patterns.

Quite apart from this, both *BEM* and the bilaterals have necessarily focused upon the "global" issues dividing churches, and have approached these in the most comprehensive theological language available. *BEM* addresses the fundamental issues of infant baptism and of baptism upon personal profession of faith ("adult" baptism); but it could make only the merest reference to the local "burning issues" of baptism in particular cultures.[79] The ultimate, universal meaning of the elements of communion is discussed with deep sensitivity. But in Pacific cultures where wine has different, largely negative connotations, can coconut milk — for them, it is argued, culturally analogous to wine in first-century Palestine — be used instead? Again, such issues could only be hinted at in *BEM*;[80] but they are of first importance to Christians around the world as they seek to live out the gospel not in the abstract, but in their own place and time.

Now the vision of unity glimpsed at the WCC New Delhi Assembly held together both the universal and local expressions of the church:

> ...the unity which is both God's will and his gift to his Church is being made visible as all in each place... are brought by the Holy Spirit into one fully committed fellowship... and... at the same time are united with the whole Christian fellowship in all places and all ages...[81]

In the present ecumenical climate it is not the "all places and all ages" which needs emphasis so much as the "all in each place". The ecumenical commitment of the churches at the international level, and the very success of *BEM* and the bilaterals, need now to be balanced by intensive work on the distinctive genius and nature of Christian faith at the local level, and the role of the local churches in the search for unity. To be quite clear: this means the local churches not only in their relation to the universal church and to the faith they confess in language common to all Christians everywhere, but precisely in their unique *local* reality: for that which makes them distinct from all other Christians everywhere else should also be brought to the search for unity.

It is here, it seems to me, that the NCCs could find a new and unifying task for the years ahead. Their vocation could be *to foster reflection on what it means for the churches to be the church in their particular place*, on the whole complex and crucial range of issues of the "contextualization" of the gospel, gospel and culture, and the construction of local theologies. They are the community of the churches rooted in a specific context. They are uniquely placed to help those churches grow together in their self-understanding *as local churches*, strengthening together their identity as the church of Jesus Christ in their unique context. And they could foster the search for unity not as a "duty" imposed upon their member churches by the world communions to which they are variously related, but as an integral expression of their own distinctive Christian life in that particular place.

This proposal might, at first sight, appear to favour those who emphasize the independence of local (national) churches over against the structures of a world communion or worldwide church. But it is not so simple. For it is sometimes the churches with the most explicit international structures which have most encouraged theological and liturgical expression in local languages and cultural idioms. And local churches which are autonomous in ecclesiological theory may yet be highly dependent on churches overseas through financial assistance, cultural and linguistic ties, material aid programmes, and patterns of leadership training.

Such a vision of the role of NCCs is, I think, in harmony with the growing common mind on the ecclesiological significance of councils of churches. Perhaps it will enrich and enliven the lives of NCCs and their member churches, not to mention the world churches and world communions to which they relate. At any rate, everyone stands to gain from a local ecumenism which is not imposed from above, but is vigorously rooted and growing in local soil. To call their member churches to such an ecumenism, to foster and struggle towards it — this is the vocation of the national councils of churches.

NOTES

[1] See the report of the "Consultation on the Significance and Contribution of Councils in the Ecumenical Movement", Venice, 15-18 February, 1982 (typescript available from the Faith and Order Commission, WCC). Recommendation IV.6 called for a "world consultation of councils of churches, sponsored by the WCC with the collaboration of the SPCU" [the Secretariat for Promoting Christian Unity of the Roman Catholic Church], "to be preceded by regional consultations...and, possibly, by a consultation of regional councils of churches organized by the WCC". The idea of regional consultations proved impracticable, but regional councils of churches were also represented at the NCCs consultation. This text is cited hereafter as "Venice Report".

[2] Victor Hayward, "A Survey of National Christian Councils", *International Review of Mission*, LX, 240, 1971, p.518.

[3] "Rethinking the Role of Christian Councils Today: a Report to Churches and Councils", report of the world consultation on Christian councils, Geneva, 28 June — 7 July 1971, Secretariat for Relationships with National and Regional Christian Councils, Geneva,

WCC, 1971, para. 13. (The Report, minus participants list, etc., was also published in *The Ecumenical Review*, XXIII, 4, 1971, pp.442-448.) (Cited hereafter as "1971 Report").

[4] *Ibid.*, para. 26.

[5] Lukas Vischer, "Christian Councils — Instruments of Ecclesial Communion", *The Ecumenical Review*, XXIV, 1, 1972, p.75.

[6] *Ibid.*, p.76.

[7] *Ibid.*, p.77.

[8] *Ibid.*, p.80.

[9] *Ibid.*, p.82.

[10] 1971 Report, *op. cit.*, para. 21.

[11] Hayward, *op. cit.*, 517.

[12] *Ecumenical Collaboration at the Regional, National and Local Levels*, Vatican City, Secretariat for Promoting Christian Unity, Typis Polyglottis Vaticanis, MCMLXXV, 4. B. c. The relevant Sections of the Report (4, "Councils of churches and Christian councils", pp.18-25; 5, "Considerations Concerning Council Membership", pp.22-26; and 6, "Pastoral and Practical Reflections for Local Ecumenical Action, pp.27-28) are published in the present volume; see pp.128-138 (cited hereafter as "Ecumenical Collaboration").

[13] Report of Workshop I: Ecclesiological Issues, world consultation of national councils of churches, Geneva, October 1986, II. 1. This text is published in the present volume; see pp.96-102. (Hereafter cited as "Workshop I").

[14] *Baptism, Eucharist and Ministry*, Faith and Order Paper No. 111, Geneva, WCC, 1982. See especially Baptism, para. 10, and Eucharist, para. 20.

[15] Johannes Cardinal Willebrands, Address to the IVth Assembly of the Caribbean Council of Churches, September 1986, typescript, p.8.

[16] This is not to deny for a moment that ecumenism at the local level is often far in advance of what the respective confessions can absorb officially.

[17] For example, the intensive discussions in New Zealand, Canada and Britain with the goal of including the Roman Catholic Church within the Council of Churches.

[18] For an account from the process towards the new ecumenical body see John Bluck, ed., *Ecumovement: Towards a new Ecumenical Body in Aotearoa*, Steering Committee of the New Ecumenical Body, Christchurch, 1986.

[19] "The Church, the Churches and the World Council of Churches: the Ecclesiological Significance of the World Council of Churches" [a statement received by the Central Committee of the WCC at its meeting in Toronto, July, 1950 and "commended for study and comment in the Churches"], *The Ecumenical Review*, III, 11, 1950, pp.47-53. The reference is to Section III. 4.

[20] *Ibid.*, III. 5.

[21] *Ibid.*, IV. 4.

[22] *Ibid.*, IV. 5. It is fascinating to compare these statements with certain texts from Vatican II.

[23] *Ibid.*, IV. 3.

[24] *Ibid.*, IV. 8.

[25] 1971 Report, *op. cit.*, para. 12.

[26] *Ibid.*, para. 6.

[27] For example: "The conciliarity which marks the life of the [Roman] Catholic Church... is based on a full and substantial communion of local churches among themselves and with the Church of Rome which presides over the whole assembly of charity." Ecumenical Collaboration, *op. cit.*, 4. A.c.

[28] For example: "The documents of the Second Vatican Council expound clearly the conviction that the unity which is the gift of Christ already exists in the [Roman] Catholic Church, although susceptible of completion and perfection." *Ibid.*, 5. a. See also 5. b.

[29] *Ibid.*, 5. a.

[30] *Ibid.*, 5. b. (i). From an ecumenical perspective this was surely the fundamental "breakthrough" of Vatican II. It is not without parallel in WCC texts: see note 22 above.

[31] *Ibid.*, 5. b. (ii).

[32] *Ibid.*, 4. A. c.

[33] *Ibid.*, 5. c.

[34] *Ibid.*, 5. d.

[35] *Ibid.*, 6. k.

[36] "An Ecclesiology of 'Councils of Churches'", typescript.

[37] *Ibid.*, p.4.

[38] *Ibid.*, p.5.

[39] *Ibid.*, pp.6-7.

[40] *Ibid.*, pp.5-6.

[41] *Ibid.*, pp.20-21.

[42] *Ibid.*, p.16.

[43] *Ibid.*, p.20.

[44] *Ibid.*, p.10.

[45] *Ibid.*, p.12.

[46] Venice report, *op. cit.*, III. 1.

[47] *Ibid.*, II. B. 4.

[48] *Ibid.*, II. A. 1 (emphasis mine). On the terms *concile* and *conseil* see note 57.

[49] *Ibid.*, II. A. 6.

[50] *Ibid.*, II. A. 14. See equally II. A. 8.

[51] *Ibid.*, II. A. 3.

[52] *Ibid.*, II. C. 2.

[53] *Ibid.*, III. 5. See also III.4.

[54] *Ibid.*, III. 6.

[55] "The Councils Serving the Churches in their Mission of Justice, Peace and Service to the World"; see the present volume, p.80.

[56] "Councils of Churches as Instruments of Unity within the One Ecumenical Movement"; see the present volume, pp.55-71 (cited hereafter as "Legrand").

[57] "Conciliar" meaning the unity of churches in full communion with one another, able to meet in "councils" analogous to those of the first Christian centuries, there to take decisions together in matters of faith, practise, and witness. This is indicated by the French word "concile"; readers will be familiar with the distinction between this and the French "conseil", covering a wide range of associations of churches and Christian groups formed for theological dialogue and reflection and, where possible in their presently divided state, common witness and action. It is this latter group which includes, of course, the national councils of churches and Christian councils generally.

[58] Legrand, *op.cit.*, p.68.

[59] *Ibid.*, p.67. Legrand is concerned about the Venice statement that the churches "provide each other with the means to grow together towards full ecclesial status" (Venice report, *op. cit.*, II. A. 4 — but quoting Tillard, *op. cit.*, pp.5-6). But while this may indeed happen in Councils, the crucial point at Venice was that the "means" come not from the council but strictly from the churches themselves.

[60] Legrand, *op. cit.*, p.61.

[61] *Ibid.*, p.62.

[62] See note 13.

[63] Koinonia, which includes as "communion" and "community" both the "vertical" and "horizontal" dimensions of ecclesiology, has been suggested as a unifying theme for much of the work of Faith and Order. This links us at once to other creative ecumenical work, not least the Study on "The Community of Women and Men in the Church" (WCC, 1977-1981).

[64] Workshop I, "The goal of unity", 3.

[65] *Ibid.*, I, "The goal of unity", 2.

[66] *Ibid.*, I, "Councils of churches and the search for unity", 4. See also III, "The unity of the church within the wider unity of humanity", 1.

[67] *Ibid.*, I, "Councils of churches and the search for unity", 4.

[68] See the discussion of Faith and Order methodology since its Montreal world conference (1963) in Thomas F. Best, "Beyond Unity in Tension. Prague: the Issues and the Experience in Ecumenical Perspective", in Thomas F. Best, ed., *Beyond Unity in Tension: Unity, Renewal and the Community of Women and Men*, Faith and Order Paper No. 138, Geneva, WCC, 1988, pp.1-33.

[69] III. "The unity of the church within the wider unity of humanity", 3.

[70] *Ibid.*, III. "The unity of the church within the wider unity of humanity", 5-6.

[71] Venice report, II. C. 2.

[72] Each church was asked to indicate "the extent to which your church can recognize in this text the faith of the Church through the ages". *Baptism, Eucharist and Ministry*, Faith and Order Paper No. 111, Geneva, WCC, 1982, p.x.

[73] Legrand, op. cit., p.58.

[74] Whether the Councils have, in fact, received adequate spiritual, psychological and material support from their member churches is another issue. See the comments on "resource sharing" — and the need for independence of councils over against "outside" funding — from the first World Consultation (1971 Report, *op. cit.*, paras. 26-27 and 29-30).

[75] Tillard, *op. cit.*, p.10.

[76] Legrand, *op. cit.*, p.68.

[77] See notes 53 and 54.

[78] Workshop I, *op. cit.*, I, Councils of churches and the search for unity, 1.

[79] See *Baptism, Eucharist and Ministry*, op. cit., Baptism, commentary on para. 21.

[80] *Ibid.*, Eucharist, commentary on para. 28.

[81] *The New Delhi Report: The Third Assembly of the World Council of Churches, 1961*, London, SCM Press Ltd., 1962, p.116.

"Ploughing the Deep Places": the Challenge to Councils of Churches

ALLAN KIRTON

Sisters and brothers, fellow participants,

I must echo the welcome to you as you attend and participate in this world consultation of national councils of churches.

You already know that I was invited to fill in here for Emilio Castro in the emergency created by the passing away of his mother-in-law and his need to fly urgently to Uruguay. The last time I saw Emilio was at about midnight on 7 September after a tropical storm had curtailed a general assembly rally in the Caribbean. He was prevented from delivering the feature address on that occasion. I never dreamed then that a peculiar twist of events would see me having to pay for that natural disaster by relieving him in the context of another! I join you in supporting that bereaved family in the fellowship of our prayers.

It is now exactly fifteen years since the last such meeting of national councils of churches took place. As I look down the list of participants at the 1971 meeting and compare it with this year's list, the very slight resemblance between the two leads one to conclude that the very heavy turnover of persons active in the ecumenical movement is visible at all levels of that movement.

There are many and varied reasons for our coming together. The formal and official one has to do with updating ourselves on the state of the movement, seeking to carry forward some of the discussions initiated in 1971 and 1982, and to explore how we can promote such relationships at all levels of the movement as would ensure greater collaboration and effectiveness.

● This is the text of the sermon preached at the opening worship of the meeting.

For three days last week, the general secretaries of seven out of the nine regional ecumenical organizations, in whose name I bring you greetings, wrestled with the many elements of our common task. Close to the end of our meeting, one of our colleagues used the word "crisis" to sum up the state of the global ecumenical landscape.

Several challenges have presented themselves. Some of them are mentioned in Victor Hayward's report on the 1971 world consultation on Christian councils; others are implied in the report of the consultation on the "Significance and Contribution of Councils of Churches in the Ecumenical Movement", held in Venice in 1982; and yet others are reflected in outlines of your presentations as well as in the topics which you yourselves have submitted for discussion.

As one listens and reads between the lines and reflects upon first-hand experience, even if the word "crisis" does not suggest itself, certainly the word "depression" does.

It is this that drives us back to the gospel. Luke records in the fifth chapter, verses 1-11, an incident which reflects disappointment and depression. The scene is a beach on Lake Gennesaret. Jesus is addressing a crowd which is growing larger by the minute. Out of the corner of his eye he can see an interesting drama which everyone else, rapt in attention to him, has probably not seen.

Some fishermen were stealthily dragging a boat on to the beach. But there is no silent way to draw a boat onto the beach. The fact that they were walking on tip-toe and almost whispering to each other as they gesticulated had nothing to do with any desire on their part not to disturb the large gathering and especially him who was on the floor.

No, this was a particularly significant scene. Peter and company, the most successful fishing enterprise on the lake, were landing without a catch. For ordinary fishermen that is nothing strange. But for Peter, James and John, their reputation was at stake. For were not James and John nicknamed because of their loud-mouthed boasting whenever they landed with their catch? No horn or conch shell was needed to attract customers! And were they not given to ribbing other fishermen who had the misfortune of coming home empty-handed?

Yes. Peter and company had to slink in without drawing attention to themselves and they had almost succeeded.

BUT JESUS HAS SEEN.

And he draws everybody's attention to them. He wants to use their boat as a temporary pulpit, and then after the teaching session, he challenges

Peter concerning his catch. With a thumping heart and a lump in his throat and an unusual lack of words, Peter admits the depressing truth: "We worked hard all night long and caught nothing."

Those of us who have been labouring in the ecumenical movement have pinpointed the difficulties and challenges — our balance sheet seems to show a deficit:

— How to retain the character of a movement while acknowledging growth into institutions — some would even say bureaucracies!
— How to respond to the widespread suspicion of and sometimes virulent attacks upon ecumenism itself.
— How to deal with the self-contradictory attitudes of the churches themselves towards councils which, to use Hayward's language, have become "the churches' alibi".
— How to come up with satisfactory mechanisms for promoting so-called "spiritual ecumenism".
— How to cope with the anti-ecumenical "new religious right" as it targets our member churches.

There are several other issues in your minds as well as those that will emerge during this week's sharing. The important thing is that some or all of these have presented themselves as intransigent challenges that will not go away.

How have people dealt with them?

1. Some have "retired hurt". They have decided that they will just not struggle any more. Having fought to the end, they have not been able to hold their ground (Eph. 6:13). They have abandoned the battle, and like Peter and his friends they wish to lick their wounds in silence. At least for their trouble they will take a sabbatical and write of the experience; many a doctoral dissertation has had its genesis in this way.

2. Some have just blamed and attacked everyone else and have sowed the seeds of discord within the movement, so that we end up fighting each other while the "principalities and powers and the rulers of darkness in high places" have a field day. This is particularly true of the reaction to the "new religious right" to which many of us have given in by accepting its definitions, and succumbed to an identity crisis in which we question the authenticity of our own faith.

3. Some have been pushed into a corner by the need to explore and come up with a satisfactory statement of the ecclesiological significance of the conciliar movement. This is not to condemn or to play down the need for such an exploration, but it is to say that the efficacy of the mechanisms which are employed as we seek to be obedient to the gospel

does not depend on our ability to find categories of dogmatic theology where they fit. The question is: Does the Holy Spirit use this mechanism, despite its probable inadequacies, for the fulfilment of the will of God? The church's creativity has often been at its highest as the church has cast its nets down in the deep places where there is risk, but where the rewards may be handsome.

4. Of course there are those who have accepted the theory that we can solve problems by talking them to death. Brothers and sisters, it remains true that if the kingdom of God depended upon the number of words we formulate, it would have come a long time ago! Our little Caribbean Conference of Churches which produces 67 pages of written material per day could have done it single-handed. Of course, the WCC would have done it long before we were even thought about! But this is not to deny the need for consulting together like this, where we can celebrate each other's victories, learn from each other's mistakes, and develop and strengthen our global ecumenical network wherein is encouragement and inspiration.

And this brings us to what appears to be Jesus' prescription for depression.

Of course, the first step is to acknowledge it without being morose about it.

The next step is to go right back to our task. "Push out your boat and let down your net for a catch" (Luke 5:4). We are told that after a plane crash the surviving flight crew is medically examined and, if cleared, is sent almost immediately on another flight. Not to do so more often than not leads to the deepening of shock and depression that might cause them never to fly again. "Get your chin up," says Jesus. Report for work immediately. In the business of the kingdom we need to hear a similar command that sends us back on duty.

The following step was that the nets were to be let down in deep water. Who knows, perhaps from his vantage point on the beach Jesus could see where the schools of fish were located. Is it not true that often, as we are bogged down by our own concerns and problems, it is impossible to see the wood for the trees? At such times we need an opportunity for regaining perspective, such as is gained from exercises like this consultation. Then Jesus sends us back to resume our task. But it is with a new command: We are to plough the *deep places*. Can it be that we are guilty of skimming the surface, of being preoccupied with the wrong things? Can it be that a part of the problem of the national councils may lie in the fact of over-concern with the pedestrian and the perfunctory? One of the remarks that I have heard made regarding NCCs is that the level of ecumenical politeness is such that no one wants to say or do anything that could possibly cause offence. Consequently, nothing that really matters, that involves risk is undertaken. Interestingly, it is when the Council, in spite of itself, is challenged from outside that it is galvanized into action and growth and trust levels begin to rise.

Finally, while Luke does not tell us the details, I believe it is safe to assume that Jesus was in the boat with them. They were, on a later occasion, to be reminded of what Jesus' presence with them could bring about. On this occasion, that presence and their trust in him made all the difference.

Our scripture reading reminds us of that. "I am the vine and you are the branches," he says. "Whoever remains in me and I in him will bear much fruit, for you can do nothing without me" (John 15:5). The fact is that apart from Jesus we can do nothing because apart from him we *are* nothing, whereas with him we achieve what he intends us to be and to do.

In this connection, let me tell you a story as I close. Actually, it is to share something I read recently in an airline magazine. It is not often that these magazines are other than dull. I suppose that they are so designed that we must be bored into a state of drowsiness!

However, this article was dealing with some research being conducted for the US space programme. Already some of the products of space research have become generally available — digital and micro-technology, for example. The research in question concerns something that is being called "magic metal". Apparently, it is an alloy whose chief property will be the ability to be moulded into any shape, melted into a crude mass, and then, under the same conditions of heat and light under which it was first moulded, it would resume its original shape. That's magic for you!

But I suppose that one needs to be careful because when this metal becomes widely used, we can be subject to numerous surprises. Consider, for example, baking the Sunday dinner when suddenly your oven becomes a Volkswagen motor-car!

However, the point is that I was very fascinated by the thought of being able to restore something to its original intended state. Human beings have moved so far away from God's original intention for us that one yearns to see their original state restored. And such magic is available and is happening daily. As the branches of the vine we are called to remain attached to Christ who is the True Vine. Is it not marvellous to know that in the light of Christ's presence and the warmth of his forgiving and restoring grace we can become what we were intended to be?

In the face of depression, therefore, coming closer to Jesus is good medicine. He helps us to lift our heads; he gives us a light in our eyes, and places a song of joy and of hope on our lips.

Amen

Councils of Churches
as Instruments of Unity
within the One Ecumenical Movement

HERVÉ LEGRAND

It gives me particular pleasure to be able to speak here, for the first time since I came into contact with the WCC fifteen years ago. I was then a member of a small joint working group of Protestant and Catholic theologians in which the Protestants were to brief representatives of the Roman Catholic Secretariat for Promoting Christian Unity on how the national councils of churches were seen from Geneva! I well remember Jacques Maury, the enthusiasm of Victor Hayward, a British Baptist who was the WCC's first secretary for national Christian councils, and Paul C. Empie, a Lutheran layman who was for many years general secretary of the National Council of Churches in the United States. I am certainly not the only person present who knew them, but I want particularly to mention them with gratitude.

I have been asked to discuss the councils of churches as instruments of unity within the one ecumenical movement. A fortnight ago I attended a consultation in Lomé (Togo) which brought together Roman Catholic lay people from four continents for an exchange of views on the vitality of their faith, in preparation for the synod on the laity to be held next year in Rome. As I listened to lay people from the three neighbouring countries of Indonesia, the Philippines and Hong Kong it quickly became clear to me that the situation of Roman Catholics in Indonesia, a predominantly Islamic society, was nothing like that of the Roman Catholic majority in the Philippines, while Hong Kong was different again. In short, I have not even tried to make my remarks today fit your personal experience, whatever that may be. For if you come from South Africa or Brazil or Eastern Europe you will be concerned with yet other worries and struggles.

● This paper has been translated from the French by the WCC Language Service.

It seemed to me that in this introductory paper for a meeting such as ours, I did not have to concern myself with evaluations or future developments. All that is foreseen in the days ahead... and no doubt you yourselves will wish to tackle your problem at greater length and in more depth once you have been able to stand back from your heavy day-to-day responsibilities.

The Venice document[1] being the only one really available to me, I shall take it as the basis for my thoughts from the ecclesiological standpoint on the role of the national councils of churches within the ecumenical movement.

My paper will be in three parts: in the first, as requested, I shall look directly at how the national councils of churches could serve unity theologically and spiritually. In the second I shall examine the ecclesiological status of the councils themselves; are they only instrumental to the church for which they are preparing, or do they already prefigure it in embryo? Lastly, in the third I shall look very briefly at the need to hold together service for the unity of humankind and service for the unity of the church.

The national councils of churches and theological and spiritual service for unity

The Venice report states that "service and unity go hand in hand" (A.11). In practice this is not always so for, according to the same report: "Many councils understand their role as primarily, if not exclusively in terms of witness and service, an understanding which has led them to minimize their role as instruments in the search for church unity" (*ibid*). The Venice report goes on to wish that there should be "more reflection on this in the life of many councils". The report is right, for if the national councils of churches (NCCs) were more closely tied into the search for unity which is intrinsic to the ecumenical movement, they could:
1) clarify the goal, that is, the unity sought by their member churches;
2) act as a link between the different doctrinal dialogues, using the means at their disposal;
3) encourage ecumenical formation;
4) care for the spiritual dimension on the road to unity;
Let us look at each of these aspects.

1. Clarifying the goal

At a certain point in a council's life it may prove useful, if not indispensable, to have an exchange of ideas on models of unity. I say *at a certain point*, because a discussion of that nature may create anxieties:

— In the early stages of cooperation it is obviously not the most appropriate topic for discussion, but it becomes pertinent when the question of growth in unity is posed by the partners.
— It is a subject which people still may be reluctant to tackle even when it is raised at the right moment, for it is reputed to be technical and difficult. Admittedly, an NCC probably cannot tackle it with the same attention to technicalities as a bilateral commission at world level, but that is no reason to reject such a study.

The question of what unity the partners may be seeking is clearly posed. There is no denying the ecclesiological differences between the member churches of a council; indeed such differences are clearly acknowledged as legitimate by the WCC "Toronto statement" of 1950:

> Membership (of a council) does not imply that each Church must regard the other member Churches as Churches in the true and full sense of the word. [2]

There are of course various strategies which can be used to avoid the difficulties inherent in discussing the unity we seek. First, the partners may try to relativize the ecclesiological questions and treat them as secondary. This strategy has no more value than any other which operates by assuming the problem had already been solved and unconsciously expecting the other partners purely and simply to adopt one's own position. Second, the partners may take refuge behind the — undeniable — fact that Christian unity will be God's gift. God will undoubtedly grant Christian unity as and how he chooses, but the churches' ignorance of how and when in no way prevents them from having some idea of Christian and ecclesial identity here and now. It will be imperfectly worked out in theory, perhaps, but is operative nonetheless. Third, the partners may choose to see the "empirical path" as the most promising, preferring to let life and experience take their course, and considering that the less said explicitly about their ecclesiological differences, the better. It is precisely to obviate this strategy that the Venice report states: "It has become clear that the goal of unity and the way to it interact upon each other."

One thing is, of course, certain: the seeds of future unity lie in the present — in the subjects selected or rejected for consideration, in the composition and representative nature of the groups working together, in working methods and decision-making. In other words, if there is indeed a relationship between the goal and the way chosen to reach it, then we cannot make do with non-explicit ecclesiologies for too long.

Since none of these "avoidance" strategies is acceptable, at least in the medium term, the member churches must be clear among themselves about the church unity they confess in the Apostles' Creed. How do they visualize unity? What value do they set on it? What are the appropriate models by which to live out that unity? The answers to these questions will show exactly how much energy the churches are prepared to put into unity and also what precise direction they are prepared to give their common efforts.

Therefore a discussion on models of unity is necessary at a certain stage in the life of a council of churches, because otherwise it would be difficult for it to be "the temporary servant of the movement towards visible unity"[3] implied in its definition.

If this is so in the medium and long term it is in the interests of healthy relations within the council that unity should be discussed even in the short term. This involves the following specific elements:

a) A council must talk about unity. If it were content simply to be a service agency and to resolve the disputes arising among its member churches, it would not be faithful to our Lord's command on the subject of unity. Secondly, it would in all likelihood be unable to function soundly because a policy of silence and evasion of the issues would probably feed the suspicions of some of its members.

b) The discussion must take place on a footing of equality. In the quest for unity each church has the right to present the conceptions it holds in the light of its confession of faith and its own historical experience. Roman Catholics were reminded of this basic rule of equality in dialogue by the Second Vatican Council (*par cum pari*, UR9). The fact that some churches have the structures of a world communion while others are national in scope does not affect this equality.

c) The New Delhi vision of unity (1961) should be the reference point. A quarter of a century after the WCC's statements in New Delhi, the NCCs cannot go back on the vision developed then:

> We believe that the unity which is both God's will and his gift to his Church is being made visible as all in each place who are baptized into Jesus Christ and confess him as Lord and Saviour are brought by the Holy Spirit into one fully committed fellowship, holding the one apostolic faith, preaching the one Gospel, breaking the one bread, joining in common prayer and having a corporate life reaching out in witness and service to all and who at the same time are united with the whole Christian fellowship in all places and all ages in such wise that ministry and members are accepted by all, and that all can act and speak together as occasion requires for the tasks to which God calls his people.[4]

This is a vision of church unity which could never make do with the "lowest common denominator", and it continues to be a driving force for unity when partial or local unions have been achieved.

d) To be dynamic, the quest for unity must set itself intermediate goals and recognize them as such. Such initial stages of partial unity which the councils can achieve more or less quickly include the following:

1. *Spiritual unity.* All ecumenical effort is spiritual in character, but spiritual unity cannot dispense with ecclesial or visible order altogether.

2. *Community of dialogue.* This is essential to re-establish unity; and it must of course also be present in the one church. But community in dialogue is obviously not yet full ecclesial unity.

3. *Community of action.* Community at this level brings into play the common service which is an indivisible part of Christian unity, but it falls short of the New Delhi vision.

4. The practice of *intercommunion* or extending of *eucharistic hospitality* among the separated churches. Of course any such practice will be challenged in councils where Orthodox, Eastern Christians or Roman Catholics are present because, as we know, those Christians see in this a failure to recognize the link they confess between communion in the faith, communion in the eucharist and ecclesial communion. For various other reasons other Christians, too, may not be satisfied with intercommunion.

As a result, spiritual unity, community in dialogue, community of action and even eucharistic hospitality, important as they are both legally and pragmatically, are still only incomplete forms of unity and do not amount to full communion.

e) If the NCCs are really to be a dynamic part of the ecumenical movement, they cannot set their sights on partial unity only, but must pursue the goal of full unity. By full unity we understand unity as described in New Delhi (see above), or else the vision we have inherited from primitive Christianity, for which the universal church is a communion of local churches, one in their diversity. This latter vision was picked up by Vatican II:

> It is in these (particular churches) and formed out of them that the one and unique Catholic Church exists.[5]

Or elsewhere:

> This multiplicity of local Churches, unified in a common effort, shows all the more resplendently the catholicity of the undivided Church.[6]

What forms can or should this communion take? Various models have been considered: organic union, corporate union, church fellowship through agreement or concord, conciliar fellowship, unity in reconciled diversity, a fellowship of sister churches.

This list of models is borrowed from the international Lutheran-Roman Catholic dialogue. I fully realize, as noted above, that they cannot be discussed in a national council with the same technicality as in a bilateral dialogue. But again I would stress that an NCC which genuinely sees itself as serving the cause of unity will sooner or later have to discuss models of unity. This discussion will enable the partners involved to clarify their goal and above all, as the Venice report says, to make more explicit the relationship between the "goal which is unity and the paths leading to it".

2. Using their own resources, to act as a link between the various doctrinal dialogues

The latest edition of the WCC *Handbook of Member Churches* states: "Churches in a council should not hesitate to examine questions of faith and order alongside their efforts to render cooperative service."[7] One aspect of this is that councils should promote an active reception of the multilateral dialogues among churches. There is almost universal recognition that the WCC Faith and Order Commission has brought new theological perspectives to the path towards unity in the faith. The study on *Baptism, Eucharist and Ministry* (BEM) is one example. A simple test of whether a council of churches is working within the unity of the ecumenical movement is to check what initiatives it has taken among its member churches to ensure that the vision and challenges contained in this document are taken into account, and to encourage the churches to study BEM and respond to it. The study under way in Faith and Order on "Confessing the Apostolic Faith Today" will probably be of equal, if not greater importance than BEM.

An evaluation of what has been done, or not done, by councils (and why) would be a valuable help towards future progress.

Councils should also promote the active reception of the bilateral dialogues in which the various member churches of a council are engaged.

Some councils already find it difficult to have any effective discussion of faith and order; the prospect of taking into account also the bilateral dialogues represents an additional difficulty. This is true in two respects: *technically*, because the multilateral dialogues have developed considerably over the past twenty years and the related documentation has now reached enormous proportions; but also *politically*, because here and there there has been, and perhaps still is, a feeling of the incompatibility of two forms of ecumenical action, namely action aimed at unity at local/ national level, and action aimed first and foremost at unity at the level of the world communions.

Indeed, certain councils of churches have felt that the failure of their plans for a national covenant could be attributed to the bilateral dialogues going on at the same time between communions at world level.

I should like, therefore, to submit the following suggestion for discussion. Precisely because of the oneness of the ecumenical movement, the national councils of churches ought also to concern themselves with the results of the bilateral dialogues in which their member churches are engaged. There are three reasons for this.

First, because there is a constant process of interaction between the multilateral and the bilateral dialogues. BEM is a good illustration: this multilateral dialogue cleared the ground for the bilateral dialogues, but at the same time itself benefited from them. This example clearly shows the oneness of the ecumenical movement: it would be unrealistic not to take into account the two types of dialogue which serve distinct but essential and complementary purposes.

Second, because the councils must be centred on their member churches. But if they gave absolute priority to realizing unity in the national context, they would then not pay sufficient attention to their member churches in their *totality* — including the ecclesiological links of those churches beyond the national level.

Admittedly, the councils have the primary duty of drawing the attention of all their member churches to their Christian responsibility in the national setting; the councils' competence is, by definition, national. But the accusations made against certain churches of "Rome-centredness" or "confessionalism", even if they were to some extent justified, would still not adequately express the legitimate ecclesiological difficulties experienced by those churches. Indeed this is why a discussion on models of unity is necessary at a given point in the life of a council; by avoiding unfounded suspicions and doubts about intentions, it enables the council really to be centred on the churches.

A discussion of this kind would reveal that visible unity at local level and visible unity at world level are not alternatives, for both relate necessarily to communion with the apostolic church and the eschatological community. Moreover, catholicity implies that the church be both one and diverse; in fact there is no universal witness which is not also local. In short, here again the oneness of the ecumenical movement obliges the councils to relate primarily to their member churches and to encourage the exchange of views between them, for otherwise the council would, in the eyes of some of its members, seem to be favouring a biased ecclesiology.

The third reason why councils should concern themselves with bilateral dialogues is that councils can play a very valuable role as a neutral third party. In national bilateral dialogues, and particularly in union negotiations, the councils of churches can be of great service to the one ecumenical movement. Whether by receiving reports of the progress of negotiations or by delegating an observer, the national councils can encourage the two partners to be more open and forward-looking in their decisions, to perhaps refrain from taking the easy way out in solving certain questions and, on other points, to set way-marks towards a wider unity.

One very practical question arises here in connection with what should ideally be done: have the national councils of churches the necessary resources to do the theological work involved in the active reception of the multilateral and bilateral dialogues? I would emphasize that the councils must encourage their member churches to respond actively, and that in these tasks there is nothing to prevent them from calling on outside resources on an ad hoc basis as required.

3. Encouraging ecumenical formation

The urgent need to encourage ecumenical formation was stressed in the fifth report of the Joint Working Group (JWG) between the Roman Catholic Church and the World Council of Churches, which stated:

> The JWG insists on the present urgency of the task of ecumenical formation. It stresses that the improved relations between still separated Christians are not enough. The scandal of Christian divisions and their deleterious effect on Christian witness continues to obscure the saving power of Christ's grace. God's plan to sum up all things in Christ requires to be shown forth in the common proclamation of the one apostolic faith and in the communion of the one visible eucharistic fellowship and to be an active power in drawing the human community into reconciliation and oneness. [8]

To do this we must first know what divides Christians; we must acquire an unreserved respect for the others' church; and we must not make light of the real differences between churches, especially when they affect daily life. But above all we must be able to explain God's action through the ecumenical movement which is gathering Christians together in unity. This implies that we must keep abreast of the recent proliferation of theological convergences and be able to grasp their significance for the life of the church.

All this requires us to be ready gradually to acquire experience of ecumenical action and be receptive to renewal. As Cardinal Willebrands said at the regional Caribbean Council of Churches, in most of our churches the training of the clergy and those with a pastoral responsibility is a crucial area for ecumenical formation. He continued:

> To speak only of the Roman Catholic Church, many good efforts are being made but much remains to be done to implement all the directives that exist concerning the training of the clergy. By way of example, can we be sure that all the priests leaving seminary have a sound knowledge of the catholic principles of ecumenism and have the firmly founded intention to assume the ecumenical responsibilities which the Roman Catholic Church recognizes as belonging to it.

Of course, it is for each church to train its own ministers and pastoral workers. But a council of churches is uniquely placed to remind church leaders of the need for an ecumenical dimension in training. Furthermore, councils may encourage or even themselves organize programmes of this kind, similar to those at Bossey but adapted to the local situation.

4. Caring for the spiritual dimension on the way to unity

The temptations to bureaucracy facing councils have been mentioned on a number of occasions (by those from Chile, for example). But even if this were not so, it is important to pay attention to the spiritual dimension on the path towards unity.

In this field, there is one action for which the councils should feel a particular responsibility, and that is the Week of Prayer of Christian Unity. This is the outstanding example of multilateral action — it includes all Christians and it is celebrated, in principle, throughout the world. It is a quite unique means of making ordinary Christians aware of the cause of Christian unity, to help them assume responsibility for it in their own sphere and take what initiatives are open to them.

The Week of Prayer is an outstanding opportunity for providing the people of God with information and spiritual and theological formation in the field of unity. But more important still is that, for a whole week, the Christians of a country gather together, visiting one another's churches in confession of the faith, praise, and willingness for conversion. As they do so they are turned together towards God, and towards his will for unity and so are open to the Christian renewal and conversion which are at the heart of the ecumenical process.

The Week of Prayer is of course not the only means the councils have to foster ecumenical spirituality. They can also support activities which will enable Christians to discover the depth of their respective liturgical traditions or, for example, arrange joint retreats for pastors from different traditions.

Though it is not the only opportunity, the Week of Prayer is still unique. It can serve as a litmus test for the national councils: Have they taken the trouble to adapt the texts they receive every year from Rome and Geneva to their local contexts? Have they been able to suggest more appropriate ways of celebrating the week, the observance of which varies around the world? Have they given any thought to how they can move from common prayer to common action and mission? From their answers to these questions the NCCs can check whether they really are an effective part of the one ecumenical movement... and can exercise their spiritual responsibility, which goes beyond the practical work of coordination which any council obviously has to do.

The ecclesiological status of the councils of churches

A number of participants have expressed the wish for some clarification of the ecclesiological status of the national councils of churches. This question will be on the agenda of a special workshop. Discussion on the subject may be useful, in that the Venice report highlights two questions which deserve further clarification. (1) Are councils to be seen as instruments of church unity or as foreshadowing it? The answer given will depend to some extent on the relationship assumed between the local church and the universal church. (2) If the councils are instruments in the service of unity, are we talking about preconciliar realities?

1. The councils: instruments or embryos?

With regard to the question whether the councils are instruments or embryos of future unity, the Venice report seems to tend clearly in favour of the first alternative. At many points the councils are described as one "instrument" amongst others — and provisional at that — of the churches' progress towards unity. For example: "It is clearly the churches themselves, and not the councils, which provide these structures (of koinonia). The task of the councils consists in preparing for these moments and exhorting the churches to make the experienced koinonia visible" (A.8). Another paragraph is still more explicit on the purely instrumental nature of the councils: "It is clear that a council, as a pre-conciliar instrument, does not bind the member churches together in full sacramental fellowship; the council as such is not responsible for Christian initiation, the administration of the sacraments, the eucharistic assembly" (A.13). Yet all Christians hold that the church is present only where the faith, and the sacraments of the faith, are to be found. The final statement in the following passage seems to clarify the purely instrumental nature of councils of churches once and for all: "The councils of churches are not the goal of the unity we seek, but a path towards that goal. ... The councils themselves are, by their very nature, provisional; they will disappear at the moment of unity" (A.14).

With these statements the Venice report adopts the line clearly set out in the report of the consultation on Christian councils (Geneva, 1971): "When churches share a common life, witness and act together, a new ecclesial reality appears, not in the council as an organization, but among the member churches sharing in this ecumenical experience through the council" (C.6).

One might ask whether the Venice report has remained equally clear and unequivocal, for in fact it sees the role of the councils as being "to allow the churches and ecclesial communities comprising it to provide each other *with the means* to grow together towards full ecclesial status" (A.4, emphasis mine). This formulation is not far removed from the idea of an "embryonic church" because, to pursue the image, in the egg which is the council, all the churches will, through one another, find full ecclesial status. The report also affirms that the councils must be able "to adapt to the constantly growing mutual recognition and to express it visibly in a more and more adequate manner" (A.6). They are an "anticipatory realization of the unity of the church" (A.15). The report also notes that in the advance towards unity "churches are able to mark irreversible steps", which "considerably strengthens the commitment of the churches... to the councils of churches" (B.4).

These statements, first of all, make it clear that the national councils of churches in themselves are considered as *special* instruments of progress towards unity (and not just one instrument amongst others). This raises critical questions from the empirical point of view: This special position is understandable in certain geographical and historical situations, but is it universally true? And even in places where the existence of councils is an established fact, are we not in some danger of deluding ourselves about their importance, in other words, their actual ability to influence parishes and theological groups?

The second thing to emerge from these statements, at least as I read them, is the impression that the Venice report wanted to go beyond the "instrumental" position adopted at Geneva in 1971. Our discussion here will no doubt bring some clarity on this point, and it is a good thing that it should be cleared up, for the instrumental understanding of the councils enables all the churches and Christian communities to belong to them, but, on the other hand, if the councils were considered to be the church of the future in embryo — membership of which would almost logically entail subscribing to a kind of irreversible "covenant" — we would then be dealing with a particular ecclesiological option. Would this not be to the detriment of the unity of the ecumenical movement? For were that indeed so, churches of the Roman Catholic or Orthodox type would find it difficult to be members, or else would be restricted and cautious in their participation.

Part of, though not all, the reservations entertained by these churches could be explained by the special position given to the local church in the search for unity. The Venice report mentions this only once in passing, in the following terms (A.3):

> It is the assembly of Christians in unity in a given place — a unity which achieves its climax in the eucharistic celebration — which is the starting point for the growth of the church of God. It is also in the local community, therefore, that the construction of unity or the common growth in unity must be rooted.

Like the Venice report itself (C.2), we must ask whether this emphasis on the local church takes sufficient account of the fact that in the New Testament, the churches in the cities, in the regions and the whole church are all called churches of God. Indeed, I would even ask if we take sufficient account of the fact that, while the local church is (at least by vocation) the church of God *in the full sense*, it is nevertheless not the *whole* church of God. To my mind, emphasis on the possible distance between the local church and the church of God, on the dialectical relationship between the local church and the universal church, would be a much more effective lever by which to encourage the local churches to join the movement towards unity. Often, as we know from experience, it is the wider communion which stirs the local churches out of their indifference or even hostility towards ecumenism. The same observation is made later in the Venice report when it states: "Sometimes the initiative (for growth into unity) comes from the highest level of responsibility (national, regional or universal)" (C.1), or again when Martin Conway emphasizes that "virtually every council of churches comes into being because of the commitment of pioneers" (III.11).

To encourage discussion, I have adopted the clear stance that the unity of the ecumenical movement will be more faithfully served by taking the instrumental view of councils. This in no way excludes councils of churches which see themselves as embryos of the church of the future. It simply means they will have less outreach because their membership will be more restricted.

Nor in describing the councils as instruments are we detracting from their importance. If they are only instruments they will not be tempted to make themselves the centre round which the churches revolve, but will centre themselves resolutely on the churches and their unity. This attitude is effective and has a certain nobility: the councils are called to disappear before that which they exist to proclaim and manifest. That, surely, is the attitude of John the Baptist, who was the precursor of Christ.

Pursuing the same image, are the councils of churches not then preconciliar realities? That is what we shall now have to look at.

2. The councils of churches as pre-conciliar realities

In a multilingual gathering such as this, there is no need to explain at length that languages are not interchangeable and that each dissects reality in its own way. That can be seen in many, many areas, even in regard to colours. Having been brought up bilingual, one of my first great surprises as a child was to discover that in my grandmother's language grass was blue! This problem worried me for days when I was about four years old — my first ecumenical experience, one might say!

Just as for a French-speaker grass is green, so for English-speakers it goes without saying that a council belongs to a "conciliar" reality. Yet that cannot be taken for granted when you are talking to people who speak French, Spanish or German. In fact English is poor here, for it has only the one word, *council*, to designate two realities between which other languages draw a careful distinction, namely:

— Councils from the Latin *concilium*, i.e. assemblies composed mainly of bishops, representing their church and necessarily in full communion in regard to the confession of faith, celebration of the sacraments, the exercise of ministry and acceptance of the ecumenical councils. These assemblies, which may be local or universal, take decisions which are binding on the churches represented.

— Councils from the Latin *consilium*, for which these European languages use a different word: these have to be clearly distinguished from the above and are consultative bodies, possibly engaging in common action. The councils of churches are a special case of the latter type of council: they by no means imply the same degree of communion as that presupposed in the ecumenical councils or regional synods, and they certainly cannot take decisions on behalf of their members. This is why, at its meeting in Accra in 1974, Faith and Order clarified the status of the councils when it stated that they "do not, obviously, conform to the definition of conciliar fellowship given at Salamanca... They might properly be described as 'pre-conciliar' bodies."[9]

In what way might the councils play a preconciliar role? In the tasks we have discussed above, i.e. by clarifying the goal to be attained (unity in communion), by fostering the reception of the results of the dialogues, by encouraging ecumenical formation and by attending to the spiritual dimension of the quest for unity. These not need be repeated here.

Yet it is highly unlikely that a council will begin its life together by this direct work to re-establish full communion among its members. Indeed, the history of the councils shows they originated much more from the desire for a common effort in Christian witness and service to society. Generally speaking, it is the creation of a council which creates a new ecclesial situation, which in turn brings its members to recognize one another as belonging to Christ because they experience that this is so in a way which is always enriching and sometimes overwhelming.

According to the Venice report (A.5), this first step in mutual recognition implies "recognizing that the others belong to Christ not simply as isolated individuals, *in spite of* the communities to which they belong, but as groups, *thanks to* the communities of which they are part". In J.M.R. Tillard's words, such recognition "demands that each reads in the other the features of one's own identity" (*ibid*).

Out of this mutual recognition and common experience in witness and service there will gradually grow the desire to resolve the divergences in faith, and then to live in full communion. In so far as councils have been able to share their experience with the people of their churches, this will in fact have been a preconciliar experience; it will have made it possible to have a foretaste of what it would be to live in unity in diversity and harmony, confessing the one same faith — the essential characteristics of conciliar life.

The Uppsala Assembly's dream and vision of a "truly ecumenical council" is thus gradually being prepared long-term in the life of the councils. We must not lose sight of this distant horizon which is a stimulus to all the churches. Although that conciliarity is in some way prefigured in the national councils of churches, they are, it seems to me, characterized not so much by "preconciliarity" as by witness and service. The two latter characteristics make the councils an illustration of the link between the unity of the church and the unity of humankind. I should like to conclude with a few brief thoughts on this subject.

The councils as active witnesses of the link between the unity of the church and the unity of humankind

The Venice report indicated that "many councils understand their role primarily, if not exclusively, in terms of witness and service" and went on to regret that this understanding "has led them to minimize their role as instruments in the search for church unity" (A.11). If this diagnosis were correct we would have grounds for concern, because that would mean a divorce between the search for church unity and the search for human unity, whereas the grand perspectives of the history of salvation invite us to link these two movements.

Jesus' purpose was to "gather into one the children of God who are scattered abroad" (John 11:52). The fathers of the church, for their part, often saw Pentecost as being at the centre of human history — with humanity scattered at Babel as we are told in the first book of the Bible, returning at that Pentecost point to the path which will bring it together as "a great multitude which no man could number, from every nation, from all tribes and peoples and tongues, standing before the throne and before the Lamb" (Rev. 7:9), as we read in the vision of the last book of the Bible.

The church thus emerges as the place where the Holy Spirit reconstitutes the broken unity of humankind. It is "…in the nature of sacrament — a sign and instrument, that is, of communion with God and unity among all men". [10] Thus, the communion of the church is the sign that the human family is called to live in unity.

That being so, it is clear that the unity of the church cannot be separate from the unity of the human community. As Cardinal Willebrands said at the fourth Assembly of the Conference of Caribbean Churches:

> While it is true that ecumenical commitment that does not issue in mission and human promotion is incomplete, social commitment that is not linked to the vision of that unity of which the Church is foretaste and sign can only run aground in the shallows of its own kind of self-affirmation.

Let us take some positive examples:
— In many countries, thanks to the national councils of churches, the press and other media have begun to talk about the Christian position or Christian commitment, without, as they once did, distinguishing between the confessions.
— Action for justice and peace has sometimes brought the churches not just to cooperate, but also to pool their resources.
— Situations where the churches have to talk to a hostile or indifferent state, or else another major religion.

As the view I am representing to you will be fairly clear, I shall not add any further examples. However, I shall end with the very serious challenge that Christian dividedness represents when it comes to testifying to the gospel in the vast world of Islam. It should be noted that for Muslims, the divisions among Christians are not a scandal of a moral sort. For them, this is a very important element in their history of salvation. Just as we Christians think that the Christian economy has replaced the Jewish one, so Muslims profess that the Mohammedan economy has replaced the Christian. Listen to what God says about this in the Qur'an, chapter 5, vv. 14 and 17:

> 14. "With those who said they were Christians we (God) made a covenant also, but they have forgotten much of what they were enjoined. Therefore We stirred among them enmity and hatred, which shall endure till the Day of Resurrection."
> 17. "Unbelievers are those who declare: 'Allah is the Messiah, the son of Mary.'"

Could it be any clearer? The reason why Christians have been rejected by God is that they have falsified the scriptures and deified Jesus Christ. The divisions of Christianity are the proof God gives to Muslims of the truth of the Qur'an. I discovered these verses while spending several years in Cairo. Obviously they did more than my grandmother's blue grass to encourage and confirm me in my ecumenical vocation.

At any rate, this reference to the Qur'an illustrates how, for hundreds of millions of Christians, Christian unity and human unity belong together.

By way of conclusion

I shall leave these thoughts on the councils of churches and their service for unity without any formal conclusion, for I am neither an expert on the councils nor a church leader. During our time here it will be for you to assess how, in your experience, they could better serve unity within the one ecumenical movement today in all its many forms.

In this evaluation process we shall learn from one another and we shall look resolutely towards the future. My remarks have been limited by my lack of experience and by the angle chosen for reflection. However, I believe I can insist on the following fact: the councils of churches are not the only place where progress towards unity is being made, but they occupy a unique position. They are at the crossroads where, generally, something of the unity of the church and the unity of the world can be forged, "that the world may believe".

It will be for you who bear the brunt of the day-to-day burden in these councils to consider how to balance the concern for church unity and the concern for the unity of the world in such a way that there can be cross-fertilization. For these councils of churches, like the church itself, stand *coram Deo*, before God, hoping that this will qualify their presence in the human community. And they stand *coram hominibus*, before and with the human community, hoping that the way in which they stand before it will also qualify the way in which they stand before God.

NOTES

[1] "Consultation on the Significance and Contribution of Councils of Churches in the Ecumenical Movement", Venice, 15-18 February 1982, mimeographed document.

[2] "The Church, the Churches and the World Council of Churches: the Ecclesiological Significance of the World Council of Churches", statement received by the Central Committee of the WCC, Toronto, 1950, printed in *The Ecumenical Review*, Vol. III, No. 1, October 1950, pp.47-53.

[3] *Handbook of Member Churches*, ed. Ans J. van der Bent, Geneva, WCC, 1985, p.4.

[4] *The New Delhi Report: the Third Assembly of the WCC 1961*, New York, Association Press, 1962, p.116.

[5] *Lumen Gentium*, 23. Cf. New Code of Canon Law, No. 368ff.

[6] *Lumen Gentium*, 23.

[7] *Op. cit.*, p.4.

[8] Published in *The Ecumenical Review*, Vol. 35, No. 2, April 1983, p.214.

[9] *Uniting in Hope*, reports and documents from the meeting of the Faith and Order Commission, Accra 1974, Faith and Order Paper No. 72, Geneva, WCC, 1975, p.114.

[10] *Lumen Gentium*, 1.

Responses
to the Address of Hervé Legrand

By Anezka Ebertova

It is not easy to review the excellent and interesting lecture of Father Prof. Legrand in a few minutes. One could review it in two ways. First, the high theoretical and theological level of the lecture could lead to a theoretical dialogue, a discussion about principles of ecumenical work, about the tasks of ecumenical councils, about the methods and models of ecumenical work, about goals and visions of the unity of Christians, and about the ecclesiastical status of ecumenical councils. The second way is to confront the principles expressed with our concrete local experience and the very varied situations of our churches, countries, societies and ecumenical councils. There is not enough time for the first way, and the second one can only be outlined in a few words reflecting our specific situation, that of the Ecumenical Council of Churches (ECC) of the Czechoslovak Socialist Republic.

Eleven of the 17 churches in our country cooperate with our ECC. Six churches and religious societies, including the Roman Catholic Church, remain outside, in spite (or maybe because) of the fact that the Roman Catholic Church represents the majority of our population. This is not simply a "negative attitude" towards ecumenical cooperation. The relations among our churches reflect a long history which has left us with ecclesiastical, denominational and social problems with difficult theoretical and practical aspects.

The preconditions for ecumenical work can be found already in the ecclesiastical conception of the first Czech reformation. This understood both the universal church and the need for catholicity, and its specific national and local forms (in which the specific "unities" share, in a distinctive way, the realization of the universal church of Christ).

However, the real beginning of our ecumenical work is closely connected with the foundation of the WCC, in which our churches took part from the very beginning. Today's ecumenical work involves appropriating the deep traditions and roots of ecumenism in our reformation, developing our ecumenical movement in connection with world ecumenism, and work in the struggle for justice, the solution of social questions and the achievement of peace. And all that is done within the modest conditions of our minority churches — that's why our work is limited as to staff and institutions.

Prof. Legrand stressed the diversity of situations and conditions under which ecumenical work is done. It is always done at a specific place and at a given time. In fact, the churches do not have an equal need and desire for unity. Some of them have in the past fought too long for their very lives and for their identity to be able to find easily an open way to cooperation. There are some difficult aspects: the fight against formalism, the efforts to move beyond official meetings of the churches' representatives to cooperation among congregations and communities, the priority given to foreign ecumenism instead of the domestic kind, and domination and ecclesiastical pride which sometimes obstruct full cooperation and do not permit the churches to be open to the questions at issue. The efforts to surmount our differences lag behind the needs of the times, and that is why we are delayed in our work of service and unity.

The lecture emphasized the role of ecumenical councils as instruments of unity. We are concerned with the level of the relations among the WCC and the world denominational bodies, the connection between the churches' bilateral relations and the broader, multilateral ecumenical work of councils of churches, and other such issues.

However, there are other factors that can contribute to understanding and unity among the churches — among them social and political factors. The structure of the society can support or obstruct ecumenism. Here it is necessary to mention the significance of the rise of the socialist society and the influence of its structure, especially on the emancipation of minority churches and theological faculties. Common tasks in service to the world and in service to peace have brought our churches together and are still a platform for cooperation in spite of the differences of denomination.

It is also necessary to stress the significance of women's contribution to ecumenism, so long as their capacity for solidarity and tolerance is not hampered by their own church leaders, who are fearful about the loss of denominational identity. The strong contribution of women has been borne out by our own experience of the work of an ecumenical group of women from our eleven cooperating churches.

The significance of ecumenical studies — both for the specific questions involved and for related issues — can also be clearly seen. "Baptism, Eucharist and Ministry" (the Lima text) is a good example of this.

In the ecumenical work of our ECC we try to achieve a balance between biblical and theological studies, between information about world ecumenism and service to the world through international ecumenical activities.

The instrumentality of ecumenical councils must be measured not only by the quantity of activities but, above all, by their effectiveness: i.e., do they change the relations among churches? Are they an instrument in service to conciliation and unity? Are they a sign of a new reality that comes into existence in the participating churches?

In reporting on our work it is necessary to stress the connection between our goals and the ways and methods of achieving them. The balance between common and individual prayers, and our activities, is a challenge to realize unity in all the necessary dimensions — the spiritual and practical ones, that of dialogue and that of the eucharist.

— Without spiritual unity our activities are formal, superficial or ineffective, or even insincere.

— Without visible cooperation, without community, without a common activity including intercommunion, spiritual unity is not profound and credible enough.

Ecumenism needs to review the criteria or qualifications for training within the various churches. What do we appreciate about other churches, what is it that we all share? What is it that separates us? In Jesus Christ we are and should be one, but Jesus did know a distinction in his work, a distinction according to the obedience to God's word, according to the willingness for penitence and conversion. We need a revision of religious and social structures according to the degree to which they realize human solidarity, service, charity and love. Don't we often prefer dogmatic, denominational, historical and ecclesiastical criteria to the criteria of spirits and gifts according to the New Testament, to the criteria of the gospel?

By La Verne Mercado

The National Council of Churches in the Philippines as an Instrument of Unity within the One Ecumenical Movement

I am not reacting directly to the presentation of Father Legrand, inasmuch as French is not my own language.[1] It was suggested that I offer some down-to-earth reflections on the theological significance of the role of the National Council of Churches in my own situation, giving examples of how the NCC serves as an instrument or tool for unity within the one ecumenical movement.

In many ways the national councils of churches are a microcosm of the World Council on the national level. This is true of our National Council in the Philippines. As such we embody the same basic theological and ecclesiological aims and bases of the "one ecumenical movement" within our own situation, and encounter some of the same theological and ecclesiological dilemmas and opportunities that the World Council encounters in its work with the churches and Christian groups around the world. We need constantly to affirm and to remind ourselves that we are not a "super" national church; we are, however, often accused or suspected by the churches of behaving like one. We base all of our work on the conviction that the church of Jesus Christ *is one* without, however, prejudging the ecclesiological problem. We do not, in other words, presume that any one conception of the church is the ground on which our work stands; neither, however, do we imply that any church's particular conception of the church is merely relative.

We are confronted by common economic, social and political issues and seek within that to bring the churches together to work out a common response. In the process of doing this, we are often accused of presenting an "ecumenical political line" that competes with and is threatening to the position that particular churches have taken. We have never negotiated unions between churches. This is something which we feel can only be done by the churches themselves acting on their own initiative. We try, however, to bring the churches together into living contact with each other and to promote dialogue and the study and discussion of issues of church unity and common action. And while we work with churches, we also work with Christian groups and movements and have had to deal with the question of whether we are a "council of churches" or a "council of movements".

We recognize, in short, that we are a fellowship of churches, not wanting the ecumenical movement to be stuck at the present status quo of the churches. At a time of grave national crisis, we are impelled to act in response to needs and issues of people who are engaged in the political struggle of our country and who call the churches in that context to give a "political shape to the hope that is within us". In the process, we are caught in the middle between those who say we are "too political" and have lost sight of our theological and religious roots, and those who accuse us of being too cautious to take concrete political options.

Thus the theological significance of our work as a national council lies in the way we localize and concretize, within a specific national situation, the ideals and work of the ecumenical movement, while at the same time bringing to the "one ecumenical movement" the peculiarities and the challenges of that specific national situation. Within this general framework, let me give three examples of how we as a Council of Churches in the Philippines serve as an instrument of unity within the one ecumenical movement.

Firstly, we bring down to the grassroots of the constituency of our churches the challenge, the possibilities and the opportunities of ecumenical discussion and action. We are presently engaged in regionalizing the work of the National Council in order to focus the ecumenical movement on the local churches. You recall that as far back as the New Delhi Assembly of the WCC (1961), the call was issued to conceive of the unity of the church as a "unity in each place". Unity, in short, cannot be conceived only in broad, universal and global terms. It needs badly to be rooted in local situations, so that the "churches around the corner" may be brought together to understand the meaning and implications of their unity in Christ in the work that they do in the places where they are. We have endeavoured to pursue this "unity in each place" right to the grassroots of our local situation by setting up regional ecumenical committees or councils in 17 regions of the Philippines.

This has led to an extraordinary increase in the degree of ecumenical consciousness and concern among a great number of people usually untouched by national programmes and events. We think that on the whole this effort is in the right direction and intend to continue developing these regional bodies as vehicles of "grassroots ecumenicity", through which the issues of church unity and the call to common action — these basic ingredients of the ecumenical enterprise — are brought to the base level of the churches.

Secondly, we are the primary conduit and mobilizational centre for our own context of the theological issues, insights and programmes that have evolved in the wider ecumenical movement. For instance, we have brought down to the level of national and regional discussion the results of the long ecumenical debate on "Baptism, Eucharist and Ministry" (BEM). The discussion of the BEM document has led us into a process of self-discovery and mutual questioning among the member churches, which has not happened before. We have also been promoting annually, together with the Roman Catholics, the observance of the Week of Prayer for Christian Unity among our churches.

We have recently also co-sponsored a joint consultation with the WCC Sub-unit on Church and Society on "New Technology, Work and the Environment".[2] The consultation looked at "technology from the underside" and provided materials that could go far in developing an Asian ecumenical perspective on such important issues as modernization, multinational corporations, the use and misuse of the natural environment, marine pollution, and the increasing trade in military technology.

We engage in joint programmes with various units of the WCC as part of our work and as part of our service and involvement in the "one ecumenical movement". In the process, we also create opportunities for discussion and interaction among ourselves on issues of critical importance to our common witness and service in our society.

Thirdly, we constantly bring the churches and Christian groups together for the exploration of their common witness and service in the context of current issues of national concern. We worked tirelessly on issues of militarization, human rights and the dismantling of the authoritarian regime of the past twenty years. We shared in the building up of "people's power" and in discerning the roots of revolution — which manifested themselves only in part in the February (1986) revolution. We worked with labour movements and peasants' organizations. We shared in the legal defence of political detainees and in providing sanctuary for victims of the dictatorial policies and practices of the deposed regime. Embarking on a new political orientation under a new government, we are now assessing the political situation in relation to the work we must continue to do. At the same time we are bringing our constituencies together to draw up our common Christian witness in what is obviously a very crucial period of our national history.

Shortly before the "snap revolution" (of 1986), we convened a consultation of "theologians" from all the member churches of the National Council to discuss together the theme "The Transformation of Church and Society". That consultation has laid the broad parameters for our present work and concerns. We talked about the massive poverty that continues to plague our national life and the life of our people. We talked about the heightening of the ideological debate in our society. We talked about violence and social change. We talked about people's movements and the involvement of the churches in them. We talked about the need for renewal among our churches. We talked about electoral and extra-electoral involvement of our constituencies. In all of these we sought the specific contribution of various confessional traditions, while trying to hammer out a common basis of common work. Despite many disagreements, it is amazing how, through serious discussion and encounter, we were able to clear the air of mutual suspicions and come up with very clear areas of common concern.

Shortly after the new government came into place, we called a consultation involving all the member churches of the National Council to formulate proposals to go into our country's new constitution. We are doing all we can, in other words, to get our churches to contribute to the formation of a new political ethos and a new constitutional framework for our country. In this consultation we came up with proposals that strongly endorsed a nationalist orientation for the new constitution. We gave support to basic land reform, to the granting of rights to workers, to the giving of free education, to the setting up of a strong human rights plank, and to the complementarity of political rights and social and economic rights. Some of our proposals have been adopted by the new constitution. Others, much to our disappointment, have been cast aside. What is important is that we have been able to mobilize our churches and other Christian groups to participate seriously in the formulation of the new basis on which our government and our political life will be run in the coming years.

Much more can be said. I would just want to underscore the conviction that national councils of churches such as ours do indeed function as a vital link in the worldwide network of the one ecumenical movement. I do not see how, without the national councils of churches, the one ecumenical movement could operate without being considered foreign to our national situation. It is imperative, therefore, that cooperation and joint work among us should continue and be improved. Thank you!

NOTES

[1] The paper by Hervé Legrand was delivered in French, with English interpretation.

[2] *Technology from the Underside*, report on the consultation on "New Technology, Work and the Environment", sponsored by the WCC Sub-unit on Church and Society and the National Council of Churches in the Philippines; published in *Tugón*, Vol. VI, No. 1, 1986, Manila, Philippines.

The Councils Serving the Churches in their Mission of Justice, Peace and Service to the World

JEAN SKUSE

Unity and the search for justice and peace go hand in hand

I begin with the basic assumption that councils of churches exist primarily to promote the unity God wills for the church. Whilst in our councils we have a variety of priorities, structures and emphases, we all have a common goal of unity within the church as a sign of the unity we long for for the whole of humanity — not that we may ever reach that goal, but we understand it as a gospel imperative for Christian discipleship "that they all may be one that the world may believe".

In the context of this goal councils are called to assist the churches in their mission to the world. Unity is not to be pursued for its own sake, but to enable churches to discern God's will and purpose for the world Christ came to redeem. It is often in the carrying out of God's mission that Christians move towards unity. As the Fifth Report of the Joint Working Group between the Roman Catholic Church and the World Council of Churches (1983) reminds us: "Today many people... receive their most significant experience of the ecumenical dimension in the common effort for justice, peace and development. Such initiatives touch on urgent problems and bring Christians together in the exercise of responsibility for building the whole human community as well as relating global issues to daily action."[1]

The urgency of the threats to survival of the whole human race, the growth of militarization, the daily struggles of the poor for food and of the homeless for shelter, the growing foreign debt of third-world countries, the attention to structural injustices and violations of human rights, prompted a response from the churches at the Sixth WCC Assembly in Vancouver (1983) to place firmly on the ecumenical agenda a priority to engage the churches in a conciliar process of mutual commitment to justice, peace and the integrity of creation.[2]

WCC general secretary Emilio Castro has stated, in the July 1986 issue of *The Ecumenical Review*: "The point of giving priority emphasis in this ecumenical process to justice, peace and the integrity of creation themselves is to insist that we may not allow internal theological or ecclesiological difficulties to be an obstacle to Christian participation in concrete struggles for justice, peace and creation."[3]

Jesus told us, if we are approaching the altar to bring our gifts to God and then remember that someone has something against us, to go and make peace with that person and then come back to offer the altar gift (Matt. 5:23-24). First, we must restore that broken relationship. The biblical concept of reconciliation, inextricably tied up with God's righteousness, is one of restoring unjust relationships. The issues of justice and peace are bound up with the issues of Christian unity, reconciliation at the altar. One cannot happen without the other. Thus ecumenical efforts to promote doctrinal agreements, or unity in mission, or a common search for justice and peace, are not competing priorities but complementary attempts to be more fully and more truly the church.

How, then, may councils serve the churches in their mission of justice and peace and service to the world?

1. Local, national, regional and world councils of churches are part of the one ecumenical movement.

This is an oft-repeated statement which must not become a cliché. While national and regional councils of churches are not members of the WCC, nor are some national councils members of regional councils, we do ourselves a disservice if we ignore this basic premise. We cannot afford to operate competitively or to distance ourselves from each other when difficulties arise. Our strength will come from assisting each other and working together to foster relationships among the churches and helping them in their mission.

While affirming the above, the report on the General Secretariat to the (WCC) Central Committee, 1984 (which recommended the holding of this consultation) warned that national and regional councils do not have an intermediary role between the churches and the WCC.[4] Councils should relate directly to member churches and member churches to councils. This is certainly true, but we should not dismiss too readily the responsibility of national councils to help in the interpretation of world and regional priorities; to provide resources to

Left, Hervé Legrand. Above, Anezka Ebertova. Above right, La Verne Mercado.

Far left, Allan Kirton. Left, Jocelyn Armstrong.

*Above left, Godofredo Boll. Above, C.F. Beyers Naudé.
Right, Jean Skuse.*

*Clockwise, from above left: Gabriel Habib, David
Bleakley, Bertrice Wood, Tunde Taylor-Thomas,
Imogene Collins and José Ivo Lorscheiter.*

member churches to assist in this interpretation; and to express solidarity in mutual concerns.

2. Councils of churches are places where churches are challenged in their denominational isolation and where appropriate ecumenical action may result.

The 1971 consultation on "Rethinking the Role of Christian Councils Today" urged "member churches to encourage their councils to pioneer on their behalf in controversial areas in which individual churches are not willing or equipped to act".[5]

As churches meet in councils, something happens which is more than each individual tradition or denomination pursuing its own agenda. An effective council will be more than the sum of its separate parts. Something radical happens when churches meet together — locally, nationally, regionally, internationally. They gain new theological insights. They become more informed. They learn from each other. They can take risks. New visions emerge. Issues too big to handle separately may be confronted together.

Of course, we all know the difficulties this sometimes creates. As Ernst Lange reminds us: "When they move in ecumenical circles, church representatives tend to talk big, to say and promise a great deal. This is not to question their personal sincerity, of course, but in the internal politics of their own churches they often find themselves in no position to redeem their ecumenical promises, or even to interpret them and enlist adequate support for them. An ecumenical maximalism and a denominational minimalism continue unreconciled side by side in the soul of one and the same church leader."[6]

Nevertheless, most churches accept this pioneering role for a council, and the decisions arrived at together influence the churches inescapably. An example of this from Australia concerns the proposed observance of a bicentennial in 1988 to celebrate the settlement of Australia. By "settlement" is meant, of course, European settlement with little reference to the Aboriginal population who have lived in Australia for more than 40,000 years.

In 1980 the Australian Council of Churches (ACC) convened a national consultation on racism as part of the series of national and regional consultations encouraged by the WCC at that time. The consultation involved Aborigines and representatives of member churches. The report, subsequently endorsed by the ACC general meeting, urged churches not to participate in any celebrations unless satisfactory progress had been made in granting of land rights to Aborigines by 1988. We seem no nearer that goal now than we were in 1980. It was a controversial decision, particularly as government money is available for local and national celebrations and the whole nation will be involved in 1988 in a series of public events. There was an attempt to woo the ACC itself with government funds to organize a national religious event. If the churches had withdrawn their support in each town, and nationally, it would have made a significant impact and the government would have been considerably embarrassed.

Member churches have differed widely in their response and none has supported fully the ACC position. Nevertheless, the issue has been put firmly on the agenda of the churches, and most denominational synods and assemblies have at least had to debate the issue; once it was on the ecumenical agenda it was also on the agenda of member churches.

3. Councils of churches help churches to acknowledge and experience the universality of the church — a vision of ecumenism which is more than local interchurch relations.

A headline in a Melbourne newspaper recently caught my eye: "Making a Big Ecumenical Splash". What was this newsworthy event? A new agreement on baptism perhaps? No, the story was about two priests, one a Roman Catholic and the other an Anglican, rowing canoes in a race across the Yarra River to raise money for charity. A Baptist minister was in a nearby boat cheering them on. The word "ecumenical" is often so trivialized that it becomes meaningless.

Ecumenism, the oikoumene, the expression which signifies the unity of the whole inhabited earth, is a symbol of something much greater than two clergy being in the same boat; much larger than the number of different denominations represented at a church service; much more than the variety of liturgical dress in a photograph; something beyond the last-minute inclusion of other churches in a denominational programme already planned.

The ecumenical themes of peace, justice and the care of creation demand that churches are more closely knit across international boundaries than ever before. As a member of a church and council that exist on an island of affluence in a sea of poverty, on a continent of security in an ocean whose peoples are under constant threat from nuclear testing and the dumping of nuclear waste, I have to be challenged to an appropriate response to the cries of the dispossessed and marginalized. The Pacific Conference of Churches provides the challenge. The problem for the people and churches in the Pacific is a problem for the people and churches in Australia. The problems in Southern Africa or Nicaragua, or Chile, or Poland are problems for us all.

In the past 18 months my involvement with the worldwide ecumenical movement has taken me to Buenos Aires (WCC Central Committee, 1985), to Rome (Joint Working Group), to the Middle East (a visit from the Australian churches), to Harare, Zimbabwe (consultation on South Africa). Whether it was walking around the Plaza de Mayo with the mothers and grandmothers of the disappeared in Argentina, or holding the hand of a woman in Beirut as she told me of her friend killed by sniper fire two days before, or discussing the paths to unity with the bishops in Rome, or listening with tears to the pleas of the black African leaders, it was evident to me, a professional ecumenist, in new and personal ways that, if one part of the church suffers, all suffer. I visited, too, at the invitation of Aborigines, the northwest town of Broome in Australia and shared once more the agony of a people dispossessed and marginalized. The churches of the world need each other if we are to make peace with the poor, bring justice to the oppressed and care for God's creation. It is a task of councils to remind the churches of this simple, yet profound, fact.

We need to find more ways of developing a constant exchange, an awareness, ways to express solidarity, processes of sharing, which characterize the universality of the oikoumene.

4. Councils are a two-way street, helping the world church listen to the local agenda.

Last year I visited a small community about 120 km south of Perth in Western Australia. I think it was the first time anyone officially representing any ecumenical council had been in the area. A person from a rural community a further 90 km away heard I was to be there and came to see me. In his hands was a copy of *BEM*. He was enthusiastic and excited about the document and wanted to talk about it. I was impressed that *BEM* had made such an impact in this seemingly remote situation. Then he challenged me.

He was a pastor to an isolated community based on a tree-felling and logging industry. Now, in protection of the environment, the industry was closing down and people would be without work. The life of the entire town would be disrupted, and the people whose families had been there for generations were to be displaced. Where could they go? What would they do? Holding *BEM* in his hands, he said: "How can I encourage my people to study *BEM* when they are so preoccupied with what is happening here? What is the relevance of the agenda of the Council of Churches to what is happening in the daily lives of these people?"

As councils we need to be more conscious of problems faced by all sections of our constituencies, to take mutual responsibility for the disruption caused in the pursuit of justice, peace and the integrity of creation. Possibly more dramatic examples would come from other countries. Maybe the experience of other places could help this community. Maybe their skills could assist others.

As each local church moves from maintaining its own life to reflecting on what it means to be the church in this place, it discovers links with other churches struggling with the same issues; it comes to an understanding of "church" which is infinitely greater, more exciting than any single congregation can perceive; it realizes that it has something to contribute to the whole church as well as something to receive from it.

5. Service to the world should be in the context of the ecumenical priorities of mutuality, justice and peace.

A parable

Once upon a time there was a small village on the edge of a river. The people there were good and so was life in the village. One day a villager noticed a baby floating down the river. The villager quickly jumped into the river and swam out to save the baby from drowning.

The next day this same villager was walking along the river bank and noticed two babies in the river. He called for help, and both babies were rescued from the swift waters. And the following day four babies were seen caught in the turbulent current. And then eight, then more, and still more.

The villagers organized themselves quickly, setting up watch towers and training teams of swimmers who could resist the swift waters and rescue babies. Rescue squads were soon working 24 hours a day. And each day the number of helpless babies floating down the river increased.

The villagers organized themselves efficiently. The rescue squads were now snatching many children each day. Groups were trained to give mouth-to-mouth resuscitation. Others prepared formulae and provided clothing for chilled babies. Many were involved in making clothing and knitting blankets. Still others provided foster homes and placement. While not all the babies could be saved, the villagers felt they were doing well to save as many as they could each day.

One day, however, someone raised the question: "But where are all these babies coming from? Who is throwing them into the river? Why? Let's organize a team to go upstream and see who's doing it." The seeming logic of the elders countered: "And if we go upstream, who will operate the rescue operations? We need every concerned person here!"

"But don't you see," cried the one lone voice, "if we find out who is throwing them in, we can stop the problem and no babies will drown. By going upstream we can eliminate the cause of the problem!"

"It's too risky."

And so the numbers of babies in the river increase daily. Those saved increase, but those who drown increase even more.

It is out of the ecumenical experience of service to the poor that the churches and councils have been prepared to "go upstream" and seek out the structural injustices which keep people in a state of poverty and powerlessness. This is a much more dangerous and a much more difficult task, and a less popular one.

The delivery of services has become a source of competition within our churches. The poor are used, sometimes, for the churches' own spiritual enhancement. Independent aid agencies, with no accountability to the churches, no mutual understanding of mission, compete for the church dollar. The funding and organization of large programmes bypassing the churches, but acting in the name of Christianity, create new power elites unrelated to local mission priorities and diverting attention from root causes of inequality.

Councils, too, must be wary of being involved in programmes which tear apart the ecumenical structures, create tension within and among member churches, and ignore the concepts of resource sharing, justice, partnership and advocacy on behalf of and in solidarity with the marginalized and oppressed.

Financial assistance must go together with involvement in the struggle to change unjust structures, and that demands commitment and solidarity. Ecumenical sharing across the divisions of the world can be a powerful sign of hope, signifying that injustice can be overcome and that fellowship and solidarity are possible. The ultimate aim of this sharing is building up a Christian community committed to justice and peace, locally and worldwide, as a sign of hope for humanity.[7]

6. Councils should reflect in their own life the unity, inclusiveness and justice they proclaim for the world.

The degree and quality of the participation of the whole people of God determine more and more the quality of the ecumenical community. Councils seek to include many groups which feel under-represented and powerless in their own churches — laity, women, youth, and those marginalized by race or poverty.

The progress towards inclusiveness is not without cost to councils of churches. As more people from further down the institutional hierarchical ladder are included, it is easier for churches who are not so inclusive to be further removed from the decisions made. Thus each new stage of inclusiveness, widening the circle so that all may come in, places new challenges before churches to be as inclusive as they expect councils of churches to be.

Our structures should also reflect wholeness. Sometimes our programmes are so fragmented and compartmentalized (e.g. into the areas of faith and order, finance, aid, refugees, church and society, education) that there is little unity in our own work. We often carry this fragmentation into our relations with other national and regional councils. Member churches, too, need to be reminded that sometimes their bilateral relationships with churches in other countries, based on historical links or continued dependencies, hinder the work of ecumenical councils in those countries. Often churches are more closely related to their missionary parents in another country than they are to other churches within their own country.

7. Widening council membership should not be a goal in itself if it is at the expense of some hard-earned gains in our ecumenical endeavours.

There is sometimes a tension between including more churches in the membership of our councils and our existing ecumenical priorities.

I need to be frank here. There are some instances at local and state (provincial) level in Australia where churches which are not members of the WCC and ACC have joined local councils. The result has been a disengagement from WCC, national and regional ecumenical programmes on the grounds that it is not right to the new members, who do not have these links, to involve them in such programmes. Similarly some of the principles of inclusiveness (women and lay) are sacrificed to include churches based on more hierarchical structures.

What is the lowest common denominator for councils of churches? The New Zealand model may have something to teach us here. As I understand it, the plans for moving to a new, more inclusive ecumenical council involve the whole people of God at all levels of the life of the churches, with the concerns of the wider ecumenical movement still firmly on the agenda.

8. Councils have a responsibility to government as well as to churches.

Our oneness in the worldwide ecumenical movement and as councils relating to each other enables us to have insights which we can share with the churches and with governments. I think, for instance, of the role the churches play in the events in South Africa, Namibia, Sri Lanka and Nicaragua and how the involvement of the churches in these countries enables councils and churches around the world, through ecumenical and other networks, to have access to information which may not be so readily available in other ways. Councils can distribute this material to government as well as church sources.

Similarly national councils have a catalytic role to play with their own governments, challenging policies and priorities and structural injustices within their own countries, seeking to find ways whereby the voices of the poor and the powerless may be heard by those in power.

Councils must beware of being compromised by governments through the acceptance of funds with strings attached or the offering of privileges. Councils should maintain a critical distance from governmental authorities. This is a much more risky role for some councils than for others. As we meet here, we know that the involvement of some of our colleagues on the staff and boards of councils of churches has meant harassment, imprisonment, torture and disappearance.

9. Councils of churches are often the focus for action groups as well as for churches.

By action groups I mean a wide range of usually locally-based ecumenical movements working for justice, peace, the environment, liberation and community. It is not surprising that such groups can sometimes identify more with the programmes of ecumenical councils than they can with their own church; they may see more of their concerns being addressed ecumenically than anywhere else.

More importantly, for the life of the churches and the ecumenical movement councils should be open to the contemporary signs of renewal coming from these sources. We should not write these groups off as being on the fringe of the church or society, but find ways to listen to and to learn from them.

10. Each council must develop a deep spiritual life as a foundation for its engagement.

There is no one ecumenical spirituality, nor even a single coherent theology in the ecumenical movement. Yet worship and intercessory prayer are at the heart of the ecumenical endeavour.

In spite of differences in tradition, each council operates with a biblically-based spirituality. The Ecumenical Prayer Cycle facilitates praying for the church in each place. Prayers for peace and justice and solidarity expressed in mutual intercessions shape our being and our doing.

Similarly our work will be enhanced if we find occasions to celebrate our life together, even if we are not yet able to celebrate it at the eucharist. Praise and thanksgiving affirm our achievements and help us discern signs of hope.

11. Councils serving the churches in their mission for justice, peace and service to the world.

This is our title and this is the crux of the matter. It is not the role of councils to do the difficult, and sometimes unpopular, tasks of the churches for them, but to challenge and enable each member church to enlarge its own understanding of mission and service to the world.

We can enumerate ways in which the agendas of world and regional councils have influenced the life and mission of churches in modern history — the changing concepts of mission, the agreements on doctrine, the relation of faith to science, the development debate, the dramatic response to refugee situations and advocacy on their behalf, the combating of racism, the challenging of international economic structures, and the concern for the integrity of creation, to name just a few. These are all convincing evidence of the contribution of ecumenism to the total life of the Christian church in recent years. All have come out of laying ourselves open to listen, to receive, to learn from each other.

The challenge for each council is to enable the ecumenical agenda to be at the heart of the churches they serve. It is to discourage them from hiving off into safe, unconnected cells — a sure sign of death and decay — but to be part of the living, pulsing organism of the body of Christ. It is to facilitate the mission of each church within the context of, and enriched by, an ecumenical dimension which is global in vision but grounded in the specific expressions of local, regional and national worship and witness.

Councils, too, are challenged to seek ways to reflect the faith and priorities of member churches, but with the added dimension of the wider ecumenical insights gained from churches and groups within the worldwide ecumenical networks.

The mission of the churches and the mission of councils are integral and integrated parts of the one mission, God's mission for the reconciliation of the church and the world.

NOTES

[1] Published in *The Ecumenical Review*, Vol. 35, No. 2, WCC, Geneva, April 1983, pp.198-218, p.215.

[2] See, for example, *Gathered for Life*, official report, Sixth Assembly of WCC, ed. David Gill, WCC, Geneva, 1983, p.89.

[3] Vol. 38, No. 3, July 1986, editorial, p.252.

[4] *Minutes of the Thirty-Sixth Meeting, Central Committee of the World Council of Churches*, WCC, Geneva, 1984, pp.22, 129ff.

[5] "Rethinking the Role of Christian Councils Today: A Report to Churches and Councils from the World Consultation on Christian Councils, 1971", WCC, Geneva, 1971, p.9.

[6] *And Yet it Moves...: Dream and Reality of the Ecumenical Movement*, transl. Edwin Robertson, Belfast, Christian Journals Limited, and Geneva, WCC, 1979, p.72.

[7] Report of the planning group for the World Consultation on Resource Sharing, WCC Executive Committee, September 1986.

Responses
to the Address of Jean Skuse

By Godofredo Boll

The situation in Brazil is that which is well-known throughout Latin America as a whole. It is characterized by centuries-long poverty and exploitation. In that situation the church is attempting to respond to the call of the poor and oppressed. Thus, in Brazil, there are grassroots communities trying to shape a just lifestyle in light of the gospel. In Latin America we have Leonardo Boff, a person who represents the ideas of liberation theology. All these things challenge the churches: how will they make a proper response to the situation? What is the role of the people in relation to our action and witness? It seems to me that for the national councils of churches the answer to these questions is connected to their self-understanding. If a council feels that it is an instrument of the churches and does not need to go beyond what they are saying — i.e. if it is cautious about assuming a prophetic role — then perhaps it will simply sum up the positions of its member churches.

For me the first thing worth discussing is how the struggle for justice and peace is part and parcel of the essence of the church. Is this struggle only a response to "the world", or is it in fact an intrinsic part of the church and of the search for church unity?

Ms Skuse used the word "reconciliation". The church, the churches and councils of churches are acting in the search for justice because they struggle and work towards a reconciled world. I would like to ask whether the foundation for that action should not be broadened, whether we should not base ourselves on the fact that God's love, which was

---

● The summaries of these oral presentations are based on notes taken by Auriol Burrows.

communicated through his Son Jesus Christ, is the fundamental and final goal of that struggle.

The other thing I would like to see discussed in our debate would be our understanding of the relation between the church and the world. I am a Lutheran and I'm afraid we Lutherans like to discuss doctrine, and to us the question of the relation between the church and the world is fundamental. We like to discuss the question of the two kingdoms. Are churches becoming so politicized that they are taking over the role proper to politicians? Where does the competence of the churches end?

I would also like to see a discussion of justice and peace from a worldwide perspective, including the question of how individual churches can complement each other and stimulate each other. Here I would say that the churches in the third world have to take up the challenges posed by churches in the first world. Today injustice prevails in the third world, and we have to see together how to achieve a more just world situation. In other words, we will find new paths towards justice and peace only when the two worlds work together to understand each other. It is also important to develop some wider initiatives; for example, in Brazil we are having discussions with the German churches about the consequences of the extensive debt in Latin American countries, particularly our own. For this is one factor that makes life difficult and makes it difficult to achieve justice.

My final point is the eschatological dimension. All our actions and struggles for justice are imperfect and partial, but as Christians we have the confidence that God will ultimately bring peace and perfect justice to the world. This sustains us in our endeavours.

By C.F. Beyers Naudé

The present struggle we are engaged in in the whole of Southern Africa is of a threefold nature. First, it is a racial struggle to remove once and for all the major and last area of racial injustice and discrimination legalized and supported by a minority regime. Second, underlying that struggle is a deeper one, the class struggle and economic exploitation challenging the churches to discover and define anew what concept of justice can apply to the exploitation of millions of people. Third is the theological struggle being engaged, not only around racism and the concept of justice as applied to the economic situation, but also with many other issues arising from our situation, e.g. civil disobedience, the legitimacy or otherwise of violence, and the question of the point at which a government becomes illegitimate in the eyes of God. In our situation, reflection on all these issues is taking place within a deeply divided Christian community.

The South African Council of Churches (SACC) has fifteen member churches representing 12 million Christians (out of a total population of 26 million). It operates through 19 regional councils (this, hopefully, will become 24, covering the whole territory), with the Roman Catholic Church as an observer. The three white Dutch Reformed churches are not members of the Council; they are excluded largely because they have chosen to exclude themselves from any meaningful type of church life, service and unity. Also excluded are the Baptist, Pentecostal and some African Independent churches. There we are, a picture of a deeply-divided body of Christ — partly reflecting the heritage of historical divisions.

In this situation the Council tries to promote justice, peace and the integrity of creation. Here I would mention the following. The Council has realized that if its voice and witness do not penetrate to the grassroots, it might as well close up shop. We do not reach the grassroots by working only through the member churches to whom we are related; but, on the other hand, what can be done can only be done via these member churches and their official structures. This creates a difficult situation and serious dangers.

The division of justice and reconciliation of the SACC has a number of field workers whose experience reflects the agony, pain, struggles, appeals, even death of our youth who tire of resolutions and want action. We are involved in the whole issue of sanctions. The SACC last year adopted a resolution appealing to the outside world to support sanctions against South Africa — it was an illegal resolution, but undergirded by a deep conviction that, unless the church is willing to face the possibility of becoming disobedient to the state, it would never give a meaningful witness to the people in their struggle for liberation and peace.

The issue of liberation theology is also strong; the kairos document has reflected clearly the deep struggle with the concept of liberation and the churches' witness to it. The document has been referred to the member churches with a request to respond by the end of this year. But the slow processes which traditionally have been set up in the church structures to get responses are one of the main problems of a council in crisis.

Another sphere is in the area of trade unions and labour. The churches in South Africa have neglected to build up meaningful contact with the workers. This is a painful and difficult process, and not understood by many in the churches; but it has to be done. The SACC has also undertaken to build up contacts with liberation movements — despite this being illegal — because we said that no solution is possible without taking into account their involvement; without them, there is no political solution for South Africa. Thus the SACC is trying to look at the future and ask itself: Is there any contribution we could make to giving guidelines from the viewpoint of the gospel? What will be the future of South Africa? What system will prevail? What clarity is there in the churches about the vision of the gospel and our understanding of what God requires of us to build a new, just, peaceful, sustainable society?

In our relationship and response to the member churches we have discovered that the tension between grassroot groups and church leadership could be very positive and meaningful, if there could be a significant dialogue involving the Council. On the issue of sanctions there are deep differences in views between us and the government, between us and non-member churches, between us and member churches. The churches are in a situation of deep conflict whenever the issue of sanctions is debated.

There is also debate on the issues raised by the kairos document, the Harare declaration, and at other points where the Council is called upon to make its contribution, theologically and otherwise. Here our minds are occupied daily by the lack of understanding and interest on the part of the churches and the labour movements. In a very specific sense, the future of South Africa will be determined by the direction which the latter will give to the country and to the church.

There is also lack of clarity and division about our response to, and relationship to, liberation movements. Here fear, self-interest and other factors play a role. How do we handle this in obedience to Christ and the gospel? The issue of what kind of alternative society we are seeking is occupying the minds of some of us. But the majority of those who have the necessary insight to make the most valuable contribution have been banned, forced underground or put in detention. So the possibility of working out the future is being delayed and destroyed by those who want to maintain their position of power.

And underlying all these issues are the different theological interpretations we struggle with: the question of violence and non-violence; the question of opposition to an unjust government, and the point when the church has to say that it no longer recognizes the government as legitimate; the concept of reconciliation; the issue of the lack of adequate theological education of the laity, from which the whole church suffers;

the issues of justice and peace, and whether they can be obtained for the whole of Southern Africa without violence.

What contribution could be made by Christian forces around the world in talking about these issues? Is it possible that a united stand could be taken about this and similar issues, so that a united voice could be heard? It is impossible for a body like the SACC to respond meaningfully without the constant fellowship, debate, discussion, and concern that has been expressed around the world, and I hope and pray that the day will come when in some small measure we will be able to return in gratitude to you what you have been giving to us. But it is also true that a special witness is being presented from our struggle to councils around the world, a witness of how we understand God's will for a people in pain, a people suffering and struggling to obtain liberation, and for a church renewed and revitalized in its witness to the world.

Report of Workshop I:
Ecclesiological Issues

I. The ecclesial nature and significance of national councils of churches

The goal of unity

1. We share the conviction of the Nairobi Assembly and the "Decree on Ecumenism" that God, Father, Son and Holy Spirit, is the foundation and dynamic of the unity of the church. This faith in the Triune God constantly calls the church to discover and reflect in its worship, life and witness the unity which is already God's gift and God's will for the church and God's purpose, in Christ, for humanity.

2. The Triune God — whose being is koinonia — calls the church to koinonia (communion, fellowship, partnership, community) in confession, worship and life. We believe that this koinonia clarifies the vision of unity which we seek and should be a matter for further theological reflection.

3. Since this koinonia makes possible our unity in diversity, councils of churches can enable differences to contribute to a richer unity while also providing the means for mutual reflection on those areas of difference which threaten to divide and to exclude.

Councils of churches and the search for unity

1. Councils of churches, as expressions of their member churches' will to unity, are given to be both instruments and signs of unity in that they can be means of enabling deeper commitment in common confession, worship and action and also a vivid expression of the growing koinonia

between the member churches pointing towards the fuller unity to which they are called.

2. Councils of churches are called to reflect and rejoice in the growing *koinonia of confession* among the churches and to encourage further reflection and action on the experience of koinonia and on matters of doctrine where there is continuing disagreement. In this process the insights and experience of the reception of *Baptism, Eucharist and Ministry* (BEM) — and of reports of bilateral and multilateral dialogues — are particularly significant as we share in the search for "A Common Expression of the Apostolic Faith Today".

3. Councils of churches are called to foster the *koinonia of worship* of their member churches, for in prayer and worship God's gift of unity is discovered. Within the councils, the churches can be challenged to discover what hinders further and fuller common worship (including the celebration of eucharist). Are the main hindrances theological, structural or human?

4. It is our experience that councils of churches are often able to discover a deeper unity when they have looked beyond themselves and have engaged together in *common witness and action*. But such common action has often required further reflection on fundamental theological issues. This essential dynamic of reflection and action, action and reflection, has enabled us to affirm that the unity of the church and the search for the unity, justice and peace of humanity belong dynamically together.

Steps towards fuller unity

We recommend:

a) that further biblical and theological reflection is initiated within NCCs on the significance of fuller koinonia within the search for unity in diversity;

b) that their member churches seek to define the implications for the national councils of churches that they are both instrument and sign of the unity we seek;

c) that national councils of churches consider their role in relation to union conversations in which member churches are engaged, and in relation to bilateral and multilateral conversations;

d) that national councils of churches encourage member churches to share insights gained from the reception of *BEM* (and other ecumenical reports) and seek ways of sharing in the process towards "A Common Expression of the Apostolic Faith Today";

e) that further consideration be given to the effectiveness of the Week of Prayer for Christian Unity as a focus for the churches' common prayer and worship;

f) that further studies be initiated of the real hindrances to fuller common worship, including intercommunion.

II. The Roman Catholic Church and national councils of churches

1. We have rejoiced in the growing participation of the Roman Catholic Church in national councils of churches throughout the world. Since 1971 the number of NCCs with full Roman Catholic membership has grown from 10 to 33. In many other places, the Roman Catholic Church has observer status. At other levels also there has been considerable development in Roman Catholic involvement in the ecumenical movement, in local councils of churches, cooperating parishes and local projects.

2. We have been encouraged by the fact that the Decree on Ecumenism and various ecumenical documents have provided a sufficient theological basis for such membership of NCCs and for common witness and action on a number of issues, particularly in relation to some critical issues within national situations.

3. We recognize that many national councils of churches have been able to make public statements when the process of agreement has been clarified. We recognize also that there are a variety of ways of dealing with such statements.

4. We have welcomed the growth in a common quest for doctrinal agreement, common sharing of spiritual life, and in common action and reflection on social and political issues.

5. We learned from some of the national councils of churches which have perceived themselves to have become more fully ecumenical precisely because the Roman Catholic Church has brought the experience and self-understanding of the unity and diversity of one world communion into the life of a national council, and that the Roman Catholic Church has been enabled to reach a fuller sense of being itself a local church in a particular place.

6. We acknowledge also that the processes of enabling fuller participation in national councils of churches by the Roman Catholic Church can be difficult for all concerned. But we believe that this whole process

enables all the churches concerned to take the national councils of churches more seriously.

We realize also that such difficulties always accompany the forging of any new relationships which open a new world for NCCs and their member churches.

7. We have recalled some of the considerations concerning council membership outlined in "Ecumenical Collaboration at the Regional, National and Local Levels" (Secretariat for Promoting Christian Unity, Rome, 1975). This document suggests various forms of local ecumenism including sharing in prayer and worship, common Bible work, joint pastoral care and shared premises. It offers guidelines for membership in national councils of churches and notes:

a) that, recognizing the ecclesial character of other Christian communities, the Roman Catholic Church has called for cooperation with other churches and ecclesial communities as such in areas of common witness and social action;

b) that councils of churches are recognized as instruments, among others, both for expressing unity and for advancing towards a greater unity;

c) that, while conversations towards union are the responsibility of the churches themselves, councils can nevertheless offer consultative and organizational assistance;

d) that public statements, which are offered by councils as a service to the churches, should be agreed through a recognized decision-making process, and their authority and validity made clear;

e) that full advantage should be taken of opportunities for collaboration in joint social action between the Roman Catholic Church and other churches within NCCs, and due regard paid to the need for theological reflection on the significance of such action for Christian witness and on those points of difference in moral teaching and understanding.

These guidelines need to become yet more widely known and recognized.

8. We have welcomed the continuing work of the Joint Working Group between the Roman Catholic Church and the WCC, at present including ecumenical formation; reflection on the issue of a hierarchy of truth; study on the local and the universal church; consideration of common pastoral issues (e.g. mixed marriages) and common social issues, and new potential sources of division (e.g. ethical questions).

9. We recommend that :

a) through the Secretariat for Promoting Christian Unity and the World Council of Churches the sharing of particular experiences of Roman Catholic Church membership in NCCs should be made possible, including examples of theological bases upon which Roman Catholic membership has become possible as well as the variety of patterns of representation;

b) NCCs and the Roman Catholic Church nationally should develop patterns of common action and witness, especially in relation to important national issues, in the knowledge that such common action often leads to a strengthening of relations and a renewed ecumenical vision; the churches also need courage to face the polarization which such common action may cause;

c) crucial theological issues in relation to the nature of the church (including, for example, the ministry of the church) should be studied more widely at national and local levels with particular reference to insights gained through the reception of *BEM*;

d) further work needs to be done on the essential questions which Protestant churches and the Roman Catholic Church need to address to each other as they search together for patterns of partnership within national councils of churches;

e) in the light of the experience gathered over recent years, national councils of churches and the Roman Catholic Church, in those areas where membership has not yet proved possible, should be given every practical encouragement to take active steps towards such membership within the guidelines already established.

III. The unity of the church within the wider unity of humanity

1. We are called to affirm the essential relatedness of the unity and renewal of the church and the unity and renewal of the human community and that there is a reciprocal dynamic to which we need to be open and sensitive.

2. God's gift to the church of koinonia is both the foundation and the liberating experience which enables the search for a fuller participation of all God's people, in all their diversity, in the life and witness of the church. We believe that this has implications for all aspects of the churches' life, including decision-making, and for the life of the world.

3. National councils of churches are called to reflect in their patterns of working this imperative towards participation, and to create a context

within which their member churches may challenge each other to explore new ways in which such fuller participation may be possible in their koinonia of confession, worship and action. We believe this to be an urgent challenge.

4. We have shared experiences of the development of such patterns of participation in a number of councils of churches throughout the world. It is essential that marginalized groups within the churches are given space to develop their own identity and are enabled to enter into fuller partnerships with others. Through such relationships all can be enriched and brought to a fuller experience of unity. Insights gained through these efforts need to be shared with other national councils of churches.

5. We have learned that national councils of churches need to develop ways of listening with sensitivity to marginalized groups both within the churches and in the wider human community as they engage together in common action in relation to particular issues and situations of marginalization. Such listening is in itself participation.

6. Within our meetings we became acutely aware that culturally-conditioned methods of working hinder the full participation of those whose cultural patterns differ. The WCC, the national councils of churches and their member churches need to develop various patterns of working, discussing and decision-making which enable and encourage fuller participation. Participation must be more than presence.

7. We were moved to hear testimony from a number of national councils of churches that they have inherited patterns of division within the church which have led to divisions in hitherto undivided human communities. National councils of churches are often called to engage in common action for reconciliation and unity in such situations. How can such councils be given fuller support in this fundamental task? We were also alerted to the danger of national councils of churches in their attitudes and actions unintentionally reinforcing forms of nationalism which deny the ecumenical vision.

IV. The significance of sociological and statistical factors in the search for unity

1. We note that, in certain areas, the majority or minority status of a church may present particular ecumenical difficulties. These often have their origins in traditional relations between churches and the state, and in

the distribution of power, influence and financial resources. These can have implications for the life and mission of the churches.

2. In these majority/minority church situations, the formation of a national council of churches is seen as both difficult and advantageous. We recommend, therefore, that any church which is a member of the WCC be encouraged to take the initiative to form a national council of churches and that the WCC be committed to assist in such situations.

3. When a national council of churches is formed in these contexts, all traditions need to be well represented. New approaches to representation will need to be explored.

4. Relationships with a majority church may be strengthened as other churches grow in unity.

Additional recommendation:

We recommend that another National Council of Churches' consultation be held outside Europe within the foreseeable future.

Report of Workshop II:
The Role of NCCs
in Promoting Ecumenism

Introduction

Like other members of the consultation, our workshop has been enriched by the opportunity to learn about one another's life and witness throughout the world. During our discussions we have gained new insights and have been enabled to relate our local work to the global situation which challenges the unity and mission of the church at this time in world history.

Our work together has been an enriching experience. We wish to share that experience by reflecting on our discussions together and by making recommendations which may enable us to improve our work at home and within the wider ecumenical movement to which we all belong.

We present our report under four main headings.

I. Relations between Roman Catholics and national councils of churches

We offer the following observations:

1. We recognize the fact that the Roman Catholic Church is now much more open to participate in national councils of churches.

2. The effects of this openness are already evident in the Roman Catholic collaboration at various levels in the social field. During the course of our discussions, we shared a variety of experiences in participation.

3. In cases where the Roman Catholic Church is not a member of the national council of churches, we offer the following comments:

a) We recognize that the Roman Catholic Church is a member in a number of national and regional councils of churches. This has opened the way for churches in a wider spectrum of the ecumenical movement to give common witness and to engage in common social action.

b) We also recognize, however, that there has been some hesitation on the part of the Roman Catholic Church in some cases, and by the member churches of a given council in others, to enter into the fellowship of the national council of churches. This arises due to a number of reasons such as:

— lack of information on what is possible at the present stage of ecumenical discussion;

— lack of enthusiasm of the leadership in a given place;

— disagreements on the understanding of the nature and function of the council in relation to member churches, etc.

Similar considerations apply to Orthodox churches in some circumstances. We hope that steps will be taken to remove the hesitations and to clarify the basis and purpose of the councils so that all the churches in a given place may enter into the fellowship of the national council of churches for witness and mission.

4. The question of the meaning of the term "council" needs to be taken into account as it might cause hesitation on the part of some churches intending to become members, including the Roman Catholic Church. We recognize the work that has been done on this subject, and we refer in particular to pp.18-26 of "Ecumenical Collaboration at Regional, National and Local Levels" (see Appendix 1) and the introduction to the 1985 revised *Handbook of Member Churches* of the WCC.

5. We welcome the fact that thirty-three national councils of churches have Roman Catholic representatives in full membership; we look forward to a continuing growth in such membership so that, together, we can proceed towards the full visible unity. We also recognize the contribution which full membership in NCCs by the Orthodox churches can bring to the move to full visible unity.

II. Ecumenical cooperation and suggested models

In our workshop, we considered the idea of sharing our strengths instead of competing with one another. This approach leads us to proclaim that for partnership really to operate, each partner needs to be seen as a whole, in full dignity.

So important is this aspect of ecumenical behaviour that we believe that there should now be a WCC desk for each region which will deal with this and allied concerns.

There is, however, encouraging evidence of a considerable degree of ecumenical cooperation. We offer the following examples:

Examples of successful cooperation and the model used

1. Lent '86, Britain: Thirty-two churches were involved in a study project on "What on earth is the church for?" This was to be done in cooperation with the local radio stations. They were all invited to a meeting, and eventually 57 radio stations cooperated in producing a series of programmes on a common theme, using some common material. Over one million people were thought to have participated, involving over 70,000 house groups.

Method: One representative from the Roman Catholic Church, one from the Church of England and one from the British Council of Churches were the joint secretaries of the wider three-year project of which this was one part. The radio side of the project was delegated to the Anglican representative who worked from his own office, using his own staff, but drawing on joint funding provided by all the denominations participating in the main three-year project. It is an example of one church working on behalf of all the others. Publicity went out through the ecumenical networks and also through the denominational networks. All churches participated.

2. Liberia: TV programme "Concern". The Liberian Council of Churches arranges a weekly TV programme on issues of general concern to the people of Liberia. Groups will suggest topics or be asked to prepare the programme. It is shown at peak viewing time (7:00 to 7:30 on a Sunday) and is very popular.

Method: This is a project of the Council of Churches, fully supported by the denominations.

3. Liberia: Roman Catholic radio station. This is owned and run by the Roman Catholic Church, but the facility is shared by other churches who can make use of it at very nominal rates.

Method: This is an example of work being done by one church and which is shared with all the others.

4. Sri Lanka: Setting up one theological college for all. This cooperation was instigated by the Council of Churches.

5. Sri Lanka: Joint Sunday school syllabus. This was worked out by a department of the National Council of Churches. This department is staffed by representatives from all denominations involved. The project was funded by WCC.

6. Christian Conference of Asia: Course for training ecumenical leaders (i.e. in-service). This is an annual event and focuses on the needs of particular types of ecumenical leaders each year.

Method: Run by the Christian Conference and advertised to national councils of churches and from there to member churches.

7. Northern Ireland: Ecumenical monastic order. The Order of St Columbanus has been set up and is fully interdenominational; it involves both men and women. It has been blessed by the denominations (including the Roman Catholic Church).

Method: No formal relationship with the NCC, but members of the NCC are in it.

8. USA, Atlanta: Training for ecumenism. Students are placed for a term in an ecumenical situation for training purposes.

Method: Nine churches are involved. There are links with the NCC.

9. Nicaragua: Joint economic enterprise in farming, etc. For example, cooperation takes place in the areas of communication, women's topics and agricultural development. Many overseas partners are involved — from united churches of the USA, German Lutherans and church groups from Norway, Sweden, Finland, Canada, the Netherlands, to mention a few.

Method: No formal council of churches, but a group from different denominations has initiated this.

10. Austria: For almost 20 years the NCC of Austria together with the Roman Catholic Church in full partnership produces a regular "Ecumenical Morning Prayer" (Ökumenische Morgenfeier) on radio every Sunday and on holidays. Each time three representatives of different churches work together as a team. They not only cooperate on common Christian concerns, but also give theological information. Yearly, about 24,000 manuscripts are sent to interested persons not only in Austria, but also in many socialist countries as well as Germany, Switzerland and Italy.

No conclusion drawn. One comment is that in developing countries, a structured and operative council of churches facilitates the receiving of funds from agencies, e.g. the WCC. In developed countries where the available funds are within the denominations, it often makes more sense to ask a denomination to work on a particular project on behalf of, and in cooperation with, other denominations, without the council of churches being formally involved.

III. National councils and relations with churches

Our discussion on this topic ranged widely, with contributions from twelve churches in five continents.

We offer the following guidelines:

1. In our NCCs we now have to talk seriously about the models of unity. The NCC is not a church itself, but an instrument which has a provisional character.

2. It is essential to have a communal element of ecumenism in the national council. The existence of the NCC is already an assuring sign of willingness to manifest Christian unity.

3. We note that ecumenism in many countries attracts a small group of people, sometimes only some of the leaders of the churches. But the number of ecumenically active people also grows all the time. We encourage churches to form NCCs where there are no councils. The way we express our faith in God may separate us, but we have to work for the issues that unite us. In some countries, NCCs receive constantly requests from local church groups for common action.

4. We note with satisfaction that NCCs can help small churches with their limited resources to get them more involved in the wider ecumenical movement, including the WCC.

5. The NCC should work for comprehensiveness while not losing the vision of visible unity. We note that visible unity is a difficult concept for some churches, and not only for the more fundamentalist churches. The NCC should enlighten all the churches about the goal of the ecumenical movement.

6. We need more personal contacts in the ecumenical movement. We also urge a more human touch in dealing with people in our ecumenical structures.

7. The question of the relationship between regional councils and national councils and smaller councils was raised, and we would recommend remedial action among those affected.

We also discussed the role of NCCs in our countries and their relationships to the member churches. The question of the role of smaller councils in the ecumenical movement was dealt with.

IV. Reasons for having councils

Having discussed the strengths and weaknesses of councils, we moved on to discuss the reasons which, we believe, lie behind the existence of national councils. These are many and varied, but we identify in particular:

1. They are primarily to promote unity between the churches. We are to be one because we understand our vocation to be one before God; it is what Christ willed.

2. Councils of churches exist to promote this unity and must never become an excuse for not moving on the road to unity or hindering that unity.

3. Unity is strength; it is helpful to speak with one voice. It is better to cooperate; our work is more effective. This is seen more acutely in situations where Christians are in a minority. Churches particularly want to unite where there is opposition.

4. They serve also as platforms. They act as catalysts and animators. They can be pressure groups and can present issues to governments.

5. Councils represent the member churches in corporate action.

6. In many countries, councils also represent the ordinary people of that country, including the non-Christian people.

7. Increasingly, the link between the people of one country and the people of another country is through the council of churches. They facilitate contact between donor agencies and specific projects. They also facilitate the donation of money (e.g. where a particular government strategy wants money to be given under specific conditions which may not always be appropriate).

8. They provide free spaces for action.

9. They help to minimalize the negative effect of continued paternalism (see point on partnership.)

10. Councils by nature respond to change and local situations. There is no single model, although they have features in common. They should be dynamic, not static.

A note on training for ecumenical work

We must do more to encourage the formation of ecumenical bodies; adequate support must be forthcoming from the WCC and regional bodies. This problem requires further study, but at this stage we suggest:

1. Specific courses should be set up, geared to the needs of NCC secretaries, possibly initially at Bossey, the Irish School of Ecumenics or the Inter-denominational Theological Center in Atlanta, USA. However, in view of the wide diversity of needs, the whole problem of curriculum content and study centres would require careful consideration.

2. Pilot schemes for intentional ecumenical learning and exchange visits specifically for NCC secretaries should be initiated in order to encourage an adequate sharing of resources. South-North and South-South movements on such a scheme should be encouraged.

3. We ask that dossiers giving stories of ecumenical learning be prepared regularly.

4. We might also explore the use of video material in the information exchange process.

Conclusion

We are well aware that there is much ground still to be covered, and we also understand that we each return home to situations which reflect a great diversity of opportunity and challenge.

But we are encouraged to discover how much we have in common and how much we have to offer one another in witness through the work of our national councils.

Above all, by being together this week and by working together we have discovered anew how relevant to God's purpose the ecumenical movement is. For all of us it has taken on new meaning.

Report of Workshop III:
Mission and Dialogue

Introduction

The initial discussion in Workshop III focused on the role of the NCCs and their member churches in the task of mission and evangelism. The members shared their experiences on their understanding of methods and objectives of mission and evangelism. There was a lively discussion on the question of re-examining our understanding of the mission of the church. Several specific issues and problems that churches and NCCs face in their task of mission emerged. Some are common theological problems shared by all Christians, whereas some are unique theological issues peculiar to a specific local, national or regional context. Considerable time was spent on identifying the mission of the church and the NCCs' involvement in it. Understanding of mission in different situations, such as in politically or religiously hostile environments or in situations where the church exists either in minority or in majority have been conditioned by these factors.

There was a lively debate on discerning some differences between the concepts of mission and proselytism. One strong view was expressed that mission does not mean usurping the pastoral role and converting members from one denomination to another. As compared to mission, evangelization implies proclamation of the gospel to those people who have not yet heard it. If evangelization is directed by one denomination to another solely for "winning souls", this amounts to proselytism or stealing members. One view was that, in spite of this risk, there was a need to re-evangelize — even by Christians not belonging to that church — such church members whose attitudes have become indifferent or merely formalistic to their Christian commitment. We call upon all churches to evangelize and work towards renewal of the congregations. Christians can and should legitimately engage in this re-evangelizing task, provided it does not involve stealing members in order to swell statistics. It was also discovered that there still is a lack of consensus on a commonly accepted definition of mission and its understanding. There are varying views on these matters among Protestant churches, Orthodox churches, the Roman Catholic Church and fundamentalist Evangelical denominations.

At a later stage in the discussion, the workshop was divided into three sub-groups, each concentrating on a narrower area, a particular aspect in relation to dialogue. Each of these groups was asked to identify specific challenges facing churches and NCCs and to look for specific strategies or models which could possibly be shared by other churches and councils.

Initial perspectives

I. DIALOGUE AND MISSION

Mission:
We note the distinction between mission in:
a) an evangelization and teaching within the church to lead members towards more active participation;
b) a going out to people who have not heard the gospel.

Dialogue:
Dialogue is a form of mission in both spheres. In dialogue, we should be sensitive to listen before speaking. As councils, we should emphasize the positive rather than the negative mission, i.e. avoid competition and participate ecumenically. Holistic mission should be undertaken, rather than polarizing towards spiritual or social mission only.

In order to decrease the gap between church and youth, churches and councils can undertake activities so that mission and dialogue can take place.

When approaching the elite as church and councils, we should be careful not to reject them before mission and dialogue.

II. DIALOGUE WITH PEOPLE OF OTHER FAITHS

In view of highly aggressive, resurgent and militant or politicized contemporary movements among other faiths, we deplore the prejudices, lopsided views, misunderstandings, questionable methods to the extent of use of violence, not only by members of any one particular faith, but of all including so-called Christian nations who perpetrate the same sins in subtler manners. We should not single out and judge, but put ourselves also with others under the judgment of God whenever and wherever we have failed our neighbours of other faiths, and seek God's forgiveness. We must be open to our neighbours of other faiths in struggles to bring about a community of people with understanding and meeting through dialogue. There is a tremendous challenge to churches and NCCs to witness through issues of peace and justice in their multi-religious environments. The methodology of doing this would in each case depend on the local situation.

III. DIALOGUE WITH PEOPLE OF VARIOUS IDEOLOGIES AND NEW RELIGIOUS MOVEMENTS

Here the question of dialogue is posed in the context of different ideologies such as Marxist, agnostic, atheistic, materialistic-capitalistic or humanistic. Any attempt to dialogue in such contexts is bound to assume some ideological dimensions. An ideology is a set of values and ways of thinking, linked to a particular social and economic context, developed to justify its own interests. Under certain circumstances, religion may become an ideology. Christians can enter into dialogue with the representatives of an ideology on the basis of a common commitment to humankind. In such a case Christians must make it clear that their actions and goals are motivated by their belief. Such a dialogue can only take place in a free environment. For Christians dialogue ends when it is no longer possible to bear Christian witness and when human values are no longer respected.

Specific issues

I. DIALOGUE AND MISSION

The sub-group on dialogue and mission was asked by the workshop to go over some other aspects of mission other than evangelism, such as dialogue as related to issues of peace and justice, and how an ecumenical body like an NCC can render witness in the context of social and economic change. The sub-group dealt with the following specific issues:
1) mission of the church to migrant and industrial workers;
2) church growth (ecumenically);
3) indigenization of the church.

1. Mission of the church to migrant and industrial workers

1.1. The group agreed that this was a global issue and also a multi-religious issue. In order to deal with this problem, we needed to identify the causes for migration, the attitude of churches in the countries from where the migrants come, and the conditions of workers in recipient countries.

WHAT CAN NCCS DO?

— Challenge member churches to face this issue ecumenically through dialogue with all parties concerned.

1.2. The group also noted that migrant workers sometimes suffer from religious intolerance. The source of the discrimination is either from religion or from government; sometimes it is both.

WHAT CAN NCCS DO?

— Some countries have study centres where these issues are studied ecumenically and practical solutions are planned cooperatively.
— Wherever possible, churches should negotiate with their own government so that the matter can be handled at government level.
— The local church should be encouraged to give pastoral care to people who are discriminated against on religious grounds in their own local areas. Also, where Christians are not accepted, we must give a positive and faithful witness to the gospel.

2. Church growth

The group made the distinction between:
— numerical growth, and
— spiritual growth, i.e. enriching of lives of people already in the church.

WHAT CAN NCCS DO?

— Encourage churches to work together in achieving these two objectives.
— Help people understand the holistic approach to mission through discussion of theological issues in seminars and groups.
— Encourage the churches to share stories of countries where the church is growing numerically and spiritually.

3. Indigenization of the church

The group would like to affirm that the indigenization is an aspect of the process of *making the church the church of the people*. It is part of mission to relate the gospel to the local people, using their own culture.

WHAT CAN NCCS DO?
— They should enable this process of indigenization to continue.
— They must take a strong position of advocacy.
— They should encourage various churches to take the first steps towards indigenization together.

The workshop added that in considering the NCCs' and churches' concern for migrant and industrial workers in the purview of dialogue, factors such as racism and racial intolerance, exploitation of migrant women, sexism and such oppressions should also be taken into account. Concern for refugees can be another area of focus in dialogue as a search for human community.

II. DIALOGUE WITH PEOPLE OF OTHER FAITHS

The sub-group on dialogue with people of other faiths dealt with the issue of how NCCs can be helpful to churches in promoting search for human community through dialogue. It was also asked that the sub-groups suggest some common responses and strategies. It was noted that in situations congenial to dialogue with neighbours of other faiths, the churches and the NCCs have been acutely made aware of challenge to unity. Interfaith dialogue implies a reflexive process, bringing Christians together to think and to do something about their own divisions before engaging in dialogue with partners of other faiths. In situations of confrontation also the NCCs have been instrumental in reminding the churches to take a united stand in their common response to the situation. It was felt that considerable difficulty is faced, not in dialogue with partners of other faiths, but rather with small and independent Christian groups who refuse to join the NCCs in their struggle for human community. It is a dilemma that these groups cannot be included in the NCCs due to their persistent refusal, and they continue to cause considerable harm and embarrassment to member churches of NCCs. However, one model which can be cited as example of a genuine search for human community are the people's movements, which may not be engaged consciously in interfaith dialogue but may involve participation of members from various religious communities.

III. DIALOGUE WITH PEOPLE OF VARIOUS IDEOLOGIES AND NEW RELIGIOUS MOVEMENTS

1. The sub-group on dialogue with people of various ideologies and new religious movements dealt mainly with questions of strategy. We

think that wherever churches support ideologies they easily run the danger of becoming an ideology themselves. We recognize that all of us are rooted in various ideological perspectives and systems, and that critical questions about the relationship of the gospel to those perspectives must always be asked. We also recognize that for many Christians the intentional use of ideological analysis of their historical and contemporary situations is one means of acquiring the skills and insights necessary for discerning the specific ways in which they may witness to the gospel in their context.

2. Advice on strategy: National councils of churches should ask the churches to keep their identity when they seem ready to affiliate with ideologies. This happens whenever a church no longer fully observes its Christian task, i.e. when it places its own interests above those of the people.

In dialogue with people of various ideologies, the church can only maintain its identity and avoid the danger of falling itself victim to ideologizing if it does not serve its own interests in dialogue but rather the interest of the people and if, in every situation, it does theology contextually.

3. Therefore, the councils should call on the churches to assume a critical attitude vis-à-vis ideologies:
a) in order to be able to judge the situation soberly;
b) in order to be able to analyze the situation jointly; and
c) in order to be able to maintain the prophetic ministry that is the church's.

It was noted that the phenomena of new cults or religious movements are of two types, i.e. sects which have arisen recently within the church, and contemporary religious movements which have arisen outside the church. One striking feature is that they are remarkably different. Some are spiritually enriching, some secretive and dangerous, some even "false", and others considerably politicized with injected ideology. Nevertheless, their existence is a reality with which churches need to come to terms. Generally churches treat them all alike — with suspicion and condemnation. Not every church can afford to respond to these in a manageable way. Only an ecumenical response is advisable and possible. Here NCCs have a significant role to play. The foremost task in this role is that of education. This task can be achieved through ecumenical cooperation. Three areas of concern can be pinpointed with regard to this issue. The phenomena of new religious movements deserve serious attention inasmuch as these claim to be the source of new spirituality relevant to our times. This claim cannot be dismissed lightly, and the best way is to approach these with the spirit of dialogue. Secondly, the question of religious freedom is involved, implying the right and freedom to propagate a new religion. Thirdly, it involves an ecumenical approach to the question of pastoral concern to those directly or indirectly involved in these phenomena.

Report of Workshop IV:
Finance, Service/Development,
Resource Sharing

Introduction

The report from this workshop group attempts to cover the subjects of finance, service/development and resource sharing as they are perceived by and related to national councils. The group, with only one woman member, was made up largely of representatives from the developing nations. To some extent, the report may therefore be seen as one-sided. However, it attempts to bring into sharper focus the struggles, needs and perspectives of the national councils concerned.

The main support of the NCCs comes from friends of the NCC, grants from missionary societies, the sale of publications, fees from seminars and training programmes, and from donor agencies located principally in the developed nations, whose mandates and guidelines are not always helpful and relevant to the contexts in which the NCCs exist and operate.

The discussions of the group touched on the following concerns as they relate to the subjects of finance, service/development and resource sharing: (1) an oppressive international economic order; (2) the relevance and role of NCCs vis-à-vis the member churches and the community; (3) the meaning of self-reliance; (4) the need for human resource development; and (5) projects and programmes, both short- and long-term, which are income-bearing. Since the national councils are links in the global ecumenical chain of interaction and mutual support, their role in addressing these concerns is vitally important, and that role needs to be continually reviewed and affirmed.

The role and relevance of NCCs

The role of NCCs in the areas of finance, service/development and resource sharing, and their relationship to member churches were reviewed. NCCs were seen and affirmed as those bodies that give meaning to the ecumenical movement and as coordinating bodies of the churches that participate in the life of the councils. There was no question of their relevance in the contemporary contexts. However, they are not to be seen as being opposed to what the member churches can do and are doing. The councils are visible manifestations of unity. The NCC is seen and appreciated as the channel through which churches themselves relate to the ecumenical family at the local, national, regional and global levels, the community, the government and other agencies.

I. Finance

Most of the councils represented in the group are to a large extent dependent on finances from abroad. This, it is hoped, will change in the future if there is a concerted effort on the part of the world ecumenical movement to influence the present economic order. The consensus of expressed opinion of the group is that the goal of NCCs is in working towards new systems of sharing of resources and self-reliance. In order for these to take place it is imperative for the NCCs to be engaged in long-term projects, some of which must be income-earning enterprises. There are several obstacles presently in the way of achieving this. Chief among these is the present economic situation in which the developing countries find themselves. Secondly, the inability of member churches to support these schemes because of the priorities that they have set for themselves and the limited funds they have at their disposal for their own programmes. Thirdly, the lack of programmes that are economically viable to produce the desired results and the lack of management expertise to sustain the projects which ensure the continuance of economically beneficial returns. Another obstacle is the acquisition of adequate funds to start such projects.

Self-reliance is not seen only in financial terms. It takes into account all other areas of the life and work of the church. It is also not to be interpreted as a state of existence that is set in opposition to interdependence. Neither must it be seen as an end in itself, but rather as a means or a channel through which meaningful sharing can take place. While it is viewed in some quarters with suspicion by member churches, the fears expressed must be put to rest because, after all, the existence of NCCs is dependent on the member churches. The achievements of NCCs bring benefit to the churches. It was felt strongly that a closer examination of the existing structures and systems of financial sharing be undertaken as soon as possible. It is evident that the present models through which present finance sharing takes place are inadequate.

II. Service and development

There are a number of ways in which NCCs can plan their services to the member churches and communities. Operational structures and financial charges vary greatly according to the choices made. In some cases historical ties make it difficult to choose the best models. There is a need to examine the systems and models by which NCCs engage themselves in this area of life and work of the councils. It was pertinent for the group to take due cognizance of what the governments may be doing in terms of service and development. In some cases there is duplication, in others the NCCs have supplemented what the respective governments are doing. Service and development programmes which are new and urgently needed are often hampered because of a lack of finances, particularly in the case of long-term programmes.

Many NCCs have set up their own development departments and programmes and have become implementing agencies carrying out programmes, including costs of the operational structures which are tailored and funded by development agencies, while at the same time running their own development projects.

The strength and organizational relevance of the NCC is to stimulate and coordinate the churches' participation in service and development as well as the spiritual renewal of the community and the search for church unity at the local and national level in terms of approach, planning and implementation. The present relevance and thrust of the NCCs in service and development is in the area of training of human resources. This is carried on at two levels. The first is directed to the needs of the churches at all levels and the second to the needs of the NCCs in upgrading and improving the skills of present personnel. The training is to include better management skills; education for stewardship and accountability; better structures and systems to allow for maximum benefits; and the formulation of better systems of sharing of resources.

One important aspect of development and service must not be lost sight of, and that is in relationship to the work that the so-called para-church and "evangelical" groups are doing. The emphasis put on projects that meet socio-economic needs may sometimes give the impression that the activities of the NCCs are one-sided. There must be a balance between these projects and the concern for the spiritual life of the churches. The link between spirituality and service and development must be brought out in all projects.

What should be noted here is that, because of the dependent nature of NCCs in most locations on funding agencies which have mandates and policies of their own, it is not always possible to fulfill the expressed needs of the churches and communities in a given area. Thus it is necessary to review partnership agreements to ensure that efforts at helping may be more mutually acceptable and beneficial.

III. Resource sharing

There is a lot of sharing going on in various ways in local and national situations. Many activities of the NCCs are in the area of sharing of human and spiritual resources, which contribute to the unity and community of the churches.

With regard to the setting of priorities and the screening of projects of the churches and the NCCs, the problems are more at the regional level than in the national organizations. The possibilities to obtain financial assistance through the ecumenical system are so limited that many NCCs have no other choice than to relate bilaterally to donor partners. The round-table structure could become a model for multilateral cooperation, but it is yet too early to know whether there could be a real change compared with the former consortia and country programme approach.

At the international level, it is hard to speak of sharing as long as the present one-way flow of financial resources dominates the relationships between donors and receivers. The churches are part of unjust economic structures. Ecumenical sharing can therefore not be seen in isolation from the search for a new international economic order. There is an urgent need for the ecumenical movement to continue to seek solutions to the injustices of the economic systems as well as to its own structures for sharing.

When NCCs function as channels for the transfer of large amounts of funds for development programmes, there is a danger that this becomes their main operation, to the detriment of their task in regard to the mission and unity of the churches. External funding can have an alienating effect on the life of the NCCs, the local churches and their relations to each other. Similarly, the power inherent in money can distort the way in which NCCs in donor countries perceive their task internally and in relation to their partners elsewhere. Money belongs to the reality of the world we live in. The insidious question of its pervading power in the ecumenical relationships has to be addressed.

The group is aware that a comprehensive report published by the WCC Office for Resource Sharing is available. Besides, a world consultation on this subject is to be convened a year from now. It is therefore expected that new models and structures for resource sharing will emerge then. With that in mind, the group felt that NCCs should be encouraged to participate in this process.

Report of Workshop V:
Councils in their Social and Political Context

Introduction

The workshop dealt with three fundamental and interconnected issues: militarization, the economic crisis, and church-state relations. In each case we used a threefold pattern of first examining the issue, then the responses and policies actually adopted by the councils and, thirdly, the implications of these for the future. For this report we have decided to use the same pattern, but to take the three issues together since they have proved in practice to be so closely connected.

We must bear witness to the value of simply hearing each other's stories. They were never remote or irrelevant; we were always speaking to each other and were directly challenged. It is impossible to reproduce these stories in this report, apart from a few minor illustrations; but we must find some way of being able to share more fully and regularly each other's experiences. The danger of generalizing or theorizing too quickly is that we lose specificity. We need to get the specifics right.

I. Recounting the effects of militarization and the economic crisis

1. The all-pervasive threat of militarization was present in all our stories, but in different ways. For some, it was primarily in the nuclear threat and the presence of bases, and the super-power confrontation. This was not confined to nations directly involved, but was seen in the Pacific, Australia and Latin America also. For others, militarization was present in ways which affected the whole quality of life — e.g. in the arms trade, in the close links of armaments to employment, research and funding; in the creation of new arms industries in third-world nations; and in the growing domination of the political scene by the military. This was seen in differing forms in the Middle East, in various Latin American coun-

tries, and perhaps most clearly in South Africa. It was also present, perhaps less obviously, in Western societies where military influence on political decisions is strong. Military bases and installations can distort the economies of many countries; they can also have direct moral and social effects, as in the growth of prostitution and drug abuse. Above all, it became clear how closely militarization and the arms race are linked with economic, political, social and cultural factors which affect the whole of life and the entire world. Psychologically, the approach to problem-solving by the readiness to destroy or dehumanize the enemy is perhaps the most dangerous consequence of militarization.

2. Closely connected is the economic crisis, resulting in extreme poverty, marginalization and injustice. In some cases this is interpreted clearly as the result of a free market world economy which makes economic judgments solely on technical grounds, and not based on human or moral values. This leads in practice to the systematic impoverishment of some and the enrichment of others and, therefore, to a clearly prophetic role for the councils. Others, while not necessarily denying this analysis, felt that there must be both cooperation within the present system to improve conditions, and to gain expert technical advice and knowledge so that the church can deal adequately with governments. This led us directly to the question of church-state relations, underlying both subjects. Our survey of these within the group produced a variety of significant stories. It is fair to say that there seems to be a growing concern in councils for peace, justice and human rights, for two reasons. Firstly, the global effect of militarization and the economic crisis becomes ever clearer; and secondly, there is an increasing sense that the gospel itself leads us to a radical encounter with every human society. This does not necessarily mean confrontation; and we recognized that in different situations the ways in which councils approach and influence governments vary greatly.

Some important questions which remain unanswered were:

— How does a state church witness?
— How do we witness in a society where all criticism is seen as political disloyalty, either because of the weakness and instability of governments, or because governments demand ideological or political conformity?
— Do we accept government funds for various programmes, or are we then in danger of accepting the system?
— What are the criteria we use in assessing the justice of our own government or state? (One suggested answer to this was the question:

"To what extent does the government permit or promote the right of some to live at the expense of others?")
— Is there a special role for the traditionally "neutral" countries and for councils in those countries?
— How do we maintain the wholeness of the gospel against those — on the political right or in the church — who would relegate religion to the area of private and family life and keep it out of the public and social sphere? How do we show this to be unbiblical?
— Do regional councils have a role in strengthening NCCs where their situation prevents them from speaking clearly on injustice?

II. NCC responses

To these issues, councils respond in a wide variety of ways. Some of these are:

1. Through prayer, worship and spirituality — special prayer events for peace were cited in the USSR, Hungary and Scotland.

2. The clear use of the Bible as the ground for our response and our concern for peace and justice. A US participant, for example, said that he always based any statement clearly on biblical symbols and texts, thus denying the use of the Bible solely to those who individualize it or to the "new right".

3. The growing need for a theology of life, as a comprehensive ground for our concern for social issues — and for justice, peace and the integrity of creation.

4. In many places, educational programmes of varying kinds seek to counter the disinformation often put out by media and governments.

5. Some have sought to strengthen NCC bilateral relationships on specific issues, e.g. between Japan and Korea on the question of Japanese immigrant policy. Joint consultations on certain specific issues have been useful, e.g. between Britain and Argentina.

6. There was an appreciation of statements of solidarity with councils in sensitive situations, as in the case of the Pacific Conference of Churches' support of the Chilean council on the issue of NASA installations on Easter Island.

7. Many councils were aware of a real attack on them in varying forms by those in power. There was a clear sense of "targeting" and surveillance — sometimes explicit but often hidden, through attempts to undermine policies or even individuals.

8. Confidence-building programmes through exchanges and visits, especially across the East-West and North-South divides, are arranged by several councils.

9. National councils or churches sometimes contribute in important ways to the international task. The Swedish Ecumenical Council has now established the Life and Peace Institute in Uppsala, while the Russian Orthodox Church has held a series of important round-table conferences on peace issues for leaders of churches and other religions.

10. We recognized several factors conditioning the councils' responses. Political conditions obviously made different responses appropriate. In some cases the churches themselves share great wealth and cannot easily identify with the poor; in others the church is facing great poverty and a diminishing minority situation (as in parts of the Middle East). In some places the rise of fundamentalist and similar groups has created new church councils, often strongly anti-ecumenical and politically conservative. In other places there have been deliberate attempts by government to weaken, divide and even destroy councils.

III. Implications for policy and joint action

1. Since the telling of the story is important in itself, we must find the means to ensure that we more fully and regularly listen to each other and learn from each other.

2. Alongside the stories, we must develop a common understanding both of what we do and why we do it. This means a theological and biblical analysis on the one hand, and a social and political analysis on the other. Each council should be asked to spell out as clearly as possible why it acts as it does in relation to social and political questions (i.e., in technical terms, its theological basis). It would be useful if councils could do this both with respect to their attitude to their own governments and with respect to their understanding of international issues which affect them.

3. We believe increased networking to be important. We understand a network to imply a grouping of two or more councils on a specific issue, and probably for a limited period. Some examples, actual or potential, would be:
— The grouping called ECCSE (Ecumenical Commission for Church and Society in Europe) which is a gathering mainly of councils in parts of Western Europe with the sole task of relating to the structures of Western Europe, i.e. the EEC, Council of Europe, European

Parliament, etc. This body must not be seen as a Western European council, but only as a network for a specific purpose.

— Similar networks might help councils relate to other multinational or supranational structures under special circumstances, e.g. when dealing with a particular multinational company or with a specific issue which involves several countries; the problem of the US threat to Nicaragua and the actions being taken on that was another example given.

— There is a felt need for more South-South networks, to strengthen councils in their specific statements or situations.

4. We need to develop positive visions and models of the alternative society we seek. This is important in local situations. We were moved by the positive vision of the future South African society which the council there is developing now. This need is international too: our experiences in every part of the world lead us to the inescapable conclusion that we must work for a new moral and social order in which economics and politics are based on moral and human standards and not purely on technical judgments.

5. Meanwhile we recognize that the wealthy and powerful industrialized countries will not easily and voluntarily relinquish their extravagant use of resources. This will happen only under increasing pressure, accompanied by the growth of enlightened self-interest. In this, too, we must plan and work together.

6. Finally, if these goals are to be achieved, the WCC itself must be seen to be less remote and closer to the councils as well as the churches. Councils need direct contact with the WCC. The regional ecumenical organizations, though of great importance in regional concerns, must not act as a filter between NCCs and the WCC.

* * *

The WCC should examine its own structure to see how it can best improve the relationships with NCCs. Since we understand the WCC's role not primarily as an agent of the churches but as an enabler and equipper, we must ask how the WCC can best enable and equip the NCCs for their tasks as outlined above. One important suggestion is that there might be a staff member in the General Secretariat of the WCC with the major responsibility of coordinating relations with NCCs. This would enable many of the suggestions above to be implemented.

The last meeting of this kind was in 1971. We hope this does not mean that the next will be in 2001! We have been greatly enriched by meeting each other and by the sense that we are *one*. We live in one world and clearly face one integrated threat to human life by the powers and principalities of death. That demands an integrated theology of life and a common strategy for the future of our world. If we cannot do that now, 2001 will probably be too late.

A Call to Ecumenical Collaboration at Regional, National and Local Levels

The following is an excerpt from the document "Ecumenical Collaboration at the Regional, National and Local Levels" published by the Vatican Secretariat for Promoting Christian Unity (1975). It is reproduced here with the permission of the Joint Working Group between the Roman Catholic Church and the World Council of Churches.

4. COUNCILS OF CHURCHES AND CHRISTIAN COUNCILS

A. Description and clarifications

a) What councils are

In various regions of the world, in different countries and even in areas of a particular country, the ecumenical relation between the Christian communities differs, and so the structures in which it finds expression also vary. In a number of places this relationship has taken the form of Christian councils and councils of churches. While these councils have their significance from the churches which take part in them, still they are very important instruments of ecumenical collaboration.

The earliest councils in the ecumenical movement were missionary councils composed of mission agencies and were formed to stimulate thinking on missionary problems and to coordinate action for the spread of the Christian message. As service agencies and other church groups took part in them, they were described as Christian councils and, finally, as councils of churches when their membership came to be composed of representatives named by the churches.

Among the principal activities of councils are joint service, the collaborative quest for a fuller unity and, to the extent possible, common witness.

Councils are multiple and diverse. Therefore theologically they must be evaluated according to their activity and according to the self-understanding they advance in their constitutions. That is to say, councils must be considered concretely as they actually exist rather than approached through theories developed concerning them.

b) Types of councils

We may distinguish the following principal types:

— *Local councils of churches* which involve the different denominations in a small area, e.g. a parish or a deanery. Such councils are not necessarily affiliated to or directed by their national council. Local councils are found in large numbers in the USA and in Great Britain.

— *State or area councils* are "at various levels below the national and above the strictly local", and their relationship to the larger and smaller councils varies; in England some of the councils of churches in the major conurbations are of this kind; and in some of these a full-time secretary acts virtually as "ecumenical officer" of the particular area.

— *National councils of churches* are composed primarily of representatives named by the churches in a country rather than of representatives from councils at a lower level.

— *Regional councils or conferences of churches* include churches from a number of neighbouring countries.

— The *World Council of Churches* is a distinct category. The World Council of Churches does invite selected national councils "to enter into working relationship as associated councils", and it has set up a Committee on National Council Relationships. This does not imply any authority or control over a particular council; in fact, the decision to enter such a relationship rests always with the national council.[1] It has to be borne in mind, too, that Catholic membership in a local, national or regional council has implications on those levels and is therefore an independent decision, separate and distinct from any decision about relationship to the World Council of Churches.

c) The meaning of conciliarity

The English word "conciliarity" can convey different meanings. For this reason Catholics need to explain what they mean by it.[2]

The conciliarity which marks the life of the Catholic Church and is sometimes expressed in ecumenical and provincial councils ("conciles")[3] is based on a full and substantial communion of local churches among themselves and with the Church of Rome which presides over the whole assembly of charity.[4] This communion finds expression in the confession of faith, the celebration of the sacraments, the exercise of the ministry and the reception of previous councils. In this sense a council is a means enabling a local church, a certain group of local churches, or all of the local churches in communion with the bishop of Rome to express the communion of the Catholic Church.

Councils of churches and Christian councils ("conseils"), however, are fellowships of churches and other Christian bodies which seek to work together, to engage in dialogue and to overcome the divisions and misunderstandings existing among them. Confessing Jesus Christ as Lord and Saviour according to the Scriptures, they engage in joint action, in a quest for unity and, to the extent that it is possible, in common witness. The fellowship which they embody does not suppose at all the same degree of communion expressed by ecumenical and provincial councils ("conciles").[5]

From this understanding it is clear that councils of churches and Christian councils ("conseils") do not in and of themselves contain in embryo the beginnings of a new Church which will replace the communion now existing within the Catholic Church. They do not claim to be churches nor do they claim authority to commission a ministry of word and sacrament.

d) Points of clarification

i) A distinction has to be made between Christian councils and councils of churches, the former including as voting members bodies and agencies other than churches.

ii) Neither Christian councils nor councils of churches are uniform in history, constitution or operation.

iii) The variety of patterns to be found in councils of churches around the world has grown up naturally; councils are autonomous bodies and no one council of churches is a sub-unit of another, nor has an attempt been made to impose uniformity. At the same time it should be noted that there are close relationships between some councils, even though they are structured in different ways.

In general terms these councils, at all levels of the churches' life, are similar in nature, but their specific functions vary according to the possibilities and needs of each level.

iv) Although the ecumenical movement calls for fellowship and collaboration at all levels, still, given the variety and autonomy of councils of churches, the decision to join a council at one level must be taken on its own merits.

Membership in local councils does not imply that membership in national councils must then be sought, just as local or national membership does not involve membership in the World Council of Churches. The question of membership must be examined separately and afresh at each level.

v) The sole formal authority of councils is that which is accorded them by the constituent members. The degree of commitment to this fellowship of churches, which a council represents, depends entirely upon the churches themselves.

vi) Councils try to make clear that as a general rule they do not have responsibility for church union negotiations, since it is well understood that these are solely the responsibility of the churches directly involved.

vii) Councils do not claim to be the only appropriate organs of church cooperation.

B. The ecumenical significance of Christian councils and councils of churches

a) The ecumenical fact of councils

The existence of councils of churches constitutes in numerous countries an ecumenical fact which the non-member churches cannot ignore and may well challenge the churches in countries where such councils do not exist.

In some places the trend towards collaboration is hastened when governments refuse to deal with a diversity of agencies in the fields of education, development and welfare and the churches engaged in these areas have to devise joint programmes.

b) The limits of ad hoc bodies for council-church relationships

In the eyes of many councils of churches, collaboration with the Catholic Church through ad hoc commissions is regarded as insufficient since this kind of collaboration:

i) gives the impression that the ecumenical fact represented by councils is not treated with sufficient seriousness, and

ii) tends to remain partial and to lack the necessary continuity.

c) The existing relation of the Catholic Church to councils of churches

The Catholic Church has full membership in national councils of churches in at least 19 countries and in a very large number of state and local councils. There is membership in one regional conference of churches covering a number of countries.[6] In addition, there is considerable Catholic collaboration with councils and certain of their programmes at various levels.

Given that "no central guidelines would be found valid for the variety of councils and of particular circumstances",[7] a number of questions and ecclesial considerations may be proposed, to be taken into account in deciding the appropriate relationship with councils.

5. CONSIDERATIONS CONCERNING COUNCIL MEMBERSHIP[8]

a) Cooperation with other churches and ecclesial communities

The documents of the Second Vatican Council expound clearly the conviction that the unity which is the gift of Christ already exists in the Catholic Church,[9] although susceptible of completion and perfection,[10] and this qualifies significantly the Catholic participation in the ecumenical movement. However, since the Second Vatican Council's recognition of the *ecclesial* character of other Christian communities,[11] the Church has frequently called upon Catholics to cooperate not only with other Christians *as individuals*, but also with other churches and ecclesial communities *as such*. This cooperation is commended both in matters of social and human concern, and even more in support of Christian testimony in the field of mission.

"Insofar as religious conditions allow, ecumenical activity should be furthered in such a way that without any appearance of indifference or of unwarranted intermingling on the one hand, or of unhealthy rivalry on the other, Catholics can cooperate in brotherly spirit with their separated brethren, according to the norms of the Decree on Ecumenism. To the extent that their beliefs are common, they can make before the nations a common profession of faith in God and Jesus Christ. They can collaborate in social and in technical projects as well as in cultural and religious ones. This cooperation should be undertaken not only among private persons but also, according to the judgement of the local Ordinary, among churches or ecclesial communities and their enterprises." (*Ad Gentes*)[12]

The documents published by the Secretariat for Promoting Christian Unity have stressed that the world often poses the same questions to all the confessions and that, in the sphere of their internal life, most Christian communions have to face similar problems. [13]

The nature of the Church, the normal exigences of the ecumenical situation, and the questions facing all Christian communions in our own day demand that the Catholic Church give positive consideration to the proper expression at every level of her ecumenical relations with other churches and ecclesial communities.

b) Implications of council membership

From a theological point of view, membership in a council of churches carries certain implications:

i) the recognition of other member churches as ecclesial communities, even though they may not be recognized as being churches in the full theological sense of the word; [14]

ii) recognition of the council of churches as an instrument, among others, both for expressing the unity already existing among the churches and also of advancing towards a greater unity and a more effective Christian witness.

Nevertheless, as the Central Committee of the World Council of Churches said at its Toronto meeting in 1950: "...membership does not imply that each church must regard the other member churches as churches in the true and full sense of the word." [15] Therefore, the entry of the Catholic Church into a body in which it would find itself on an equal footing with other bodies which also claim to be churches would not diminish its faith about its uniqueness. The Second Vatican Council has clearly stated that the unique Church of Christ "constituted and organized in the world as a society subsists in the Catholic Church which is governed by the successor of Peter and the bishops in communion with that successor, although many elements of sanctification and of truth can be found outside of her visible structure." [16]

c) Councils and Christian unity

Some councils of churches are not themselves churches, they do not assume the responsibility of acting for churches which are contemplating or have begun to engage in unity conversations. In principle, their action is in the practical field. However, because of their facilities and their administrative resources, they are in a position to give important material help and can, upon request of the churches concerned, give consultative and organizational assistance. While the study of "Faith and Order" questions, which goes on under the auspices of many councils and is authorized by member churches, has a deep importance in stimulating member churches to a deeper understanding of the demands of the unity willed by Christ, and to facing old deadlocks in a new way, nevertheless it is not the task of a council to take the initiative in promoting formal doctrinal conversations between churches. These belong properly to the immediate and bilateral contacts between churches.

d) The problem of council statements

Councils of churches, in some cases more frequently than the member churches themselves, on occasion make public statements on issues of common concern. These are addressed more often to areas of social justice, human development, general welfare, and public or private morality. They are based on theological positions that may or may not be articulated themselves. Unless explicitly authorized, they cannot be considered as official utterances on behalf of the churches but are offered as a service to the churches. They are often directed also to the wider public or even to specific audiences, such as government authorities. They vary in character from broad statements of position or orientation in general areas to specific stands on concrete questions. In some instances they examine and illuminate a subject, identifying a number of possible approaches rather than adopting a position. This practice of making statements has caused concern in some churches and calls especially for clarification where the Catholic Church considers the possibility of membership in councils of churches.

i) The decision-making process

In attempting to fix criteria to evaluate the deliberative process in a particular council, it will be necessary to give serious consideration to the hesitations and objections of its members. A common declaration which engages the moral responsibility of its members is possible only with the consent of all.

ii) The authority and use of public statements

Important as is the process by which statements are formulated and issued, equally important is the manner in which they are received — both by the individual members of the churches and by the public at large. Differences in the weight of authority given to official statements within member churches, as well as differences in the normal mode of formulation and issuance of statements, can result in serious difficulties. Efforts have to be made to obviate the confusion that may arise in practice. Such statements should clearly identify the theological principles on which they are based so as to facilitate their acceptance by church members as being in accord with their own Christian commitment. Since councils cannot usurp the position of the churches that comprise their membership, they need to study how best they can determine what matters fall within their own purpose and mandate and to be sure of the approval of member churches before publishing statements.

iii) Regard for minority viewpoints

Councils, being composed of separated churches, inevitably face issues on which they cannot reach a perfect consensus. A profound respect for the integrity and individuality of its member churches will lead a council to develop procedures for ensuring that a minority dissent will be adequately expressed for the mutual benefit of the council, its members, and all to whom the council speaks. Provisions have to be made within councils for such expression of minority viewpoints, and in this context polarization ought to be avoided.

e) Joint social action — opportunities and problems

i) In the Apostolic Letter *Octogesima Adveniens*, the Holy Father has written: "It is up to these Christian communities, with the help of the Holy Spirit, in communion with the bishops who hold responsibility, and in dialogue with other Christian brethren and all men of good will, to discern the options and commitments which are called for in order to bring about the social, political and economic changes seen in many cases to be urgently needed" (n.4).

ii) At a number of points Christian positions permit and encourage collaboration with other spiritual and ideological families. Therefore, councils and ecumenical organizations rightly pay serious attention to possible areas of collaboration (e.g. in the field of development, housing, health, and various forms of relief) which concern people of other living faiths as well as Christian churches and ecclesial communities.

iii) Christian social action to which many councils of churches and ecumenical bodies devote a large part of their endeavours also raises questions of theological reflection. In the first place, there is the essential role of social action in the proclamation of the Gospel. "Action on behalf of justice and participation in the transformation of the world fully appear to us as a constitutive dimension of the preaching of the Gospel or, in other words, of the Church's mission for the redemption of the human race and its liberation from every oppressive situation."[17]

Further, there are questions of morality, especially regarding family life, which more and more need to be faced seriously in all their complexity, in particular those which concern population, family life, marriage, contraception, abortion, euthanasia and others. These questions need to be studied with due regard to the moral teachings of the churches concerned and above all taking into account the objective content of Catholic ethics.[18]

6. PASTORAL AND PRACTICAL REFLECTIONS FOR LOCAL ECUMENICAL ACTION

a) Full account ought to be given to local needs and problems in organizing ecumenical action; models from other places cannot simply be imitated.

b) Ultimately, it is always the responsibility of the regional or national episcopal conference to decide on the acceptability and the appropriateness of all forms of local ecumenical action. They should do this in cooperation with the appropriate organ of the Holy See, viz. the Secretariat for Promoting Christian Unity.

c) What really matters is not the creation of new structures but the collaboration of Christians in prayer, reflection and action, based on common baptism and on a faith which on many essential points is also common.

d) Sometimes the best form of collaboration may be for one church and ecclesial community to participate fully in the programmes already set up by another. At other times parallel coordinated action and the joint use of the results may be more appropriate. In any event, as collaboration becomes closer, a simplification of structures should be sought and unnecessary multiplication of structures avoided.

e) Where joint action or programmes are decided on, they ought to be undertaken fully by both sides and duly authorized by the respective authorities right from the earliest stages of planning.

f) It is necessary that where there are regional, national and local doctrinal bilateral dialogues, episcopal conferences ensure that at the right time there is contact with the Holy See.

g) Among the many forms of ecumenical cooperation, councils of churches and Christian councils are not the only form but they are certainly one of the more important. Since regional, national and local councils are widespread in many parts of the world and do play an important role in ecumenical relations, the responsible contacts which the Catholic Church is having with them are welcome.

h) It is normal that councils should want to discuss and reflect upon the doctrinal bases of the practical projects they undertake. But in such cases it is important to clarify the doctrinal principles involved. It should always be clear that when Catholics take part in a council, they can enter into such discussions only in conformity with the teaching of their Church.

i) The first and immediate responsibility for a decision to join a council rests with the highest ecclesiastical authority in the area served by the council. In practical terms this responsibility is not transferable. With regard to national councils, the authority would generally be the episcopal conference (where there is only one diocese for the nation, it would be the Ordinary of the diocese). In reaching a decision, there must necessarily be communication with the Secretariat for Promoting Christian Unity.

j) The degree of involvement of different confessions in the same council depends directly on their respective structures, especially in those things concerning the nature and exercise of authority. However, it would seem desirable that councils be constituted in such a way that the various members can all accept the full measure of involvement possible for them.

k) Membership in a council is a serious responsibility of the Catholic bishops or their delegates. It is necessary that the Catholic representatives in councils should be personally qualified and, while representing the Church on matters within their competence, they should be clearly aware of the limits beyond which they cannot commit the Church without prior reference to higher authority.

l) It is not enough that the Church simply have delegates in a council or other ecumenical structure; unless they are taken seriously by the Catholic authorities, the Catholic participation will remain purely superficial. For the same reason all participation in ecumenical structures should be accompanied by constant ecumenical education of Catholics concerning the implications of such participation.

NOTES

[1] Cf. the *New Delhi Report* (London, 1962). Appendix II, XI, p.438.

[2] The understanding not only of Catholics but of Orthodox, Anglicans and many Protestants finds expression in the description of "conciliarity" given in a paper of the Salamanca Conference (1973) of the WCC Faith and Order Commission.

[3] In some languages other than English two distinct words are used to denote the realities for which in English the single word "council" is used. In French, for example, there are the

words "concile" and "conseil"; in Italian "concilio" and "consiglio"; in Spanish "concilio" and "consejo"; in German "Konzil" and "Rat"; and in Latin "concilium" and "consilium".

[4] Cf. *Lumen Gentium*, 13; *Ad Gentes*, 22; S. Ignatius M., *Ad Rom*, Praef.

[5] In the meeting of the Faith and Order Commission of the WCC held in Accra, 1974, the following comment was made: "The local, national and world councils of churches which perform such a vital role in the modern ecumenical movement do not, obviously, conform to the definition of conciliar fellowship given at Salamanca. They are federal in character and do not enjoy either the full communion or the capacity to make decisions for all their members. They might properly be described as *'pre-conciliar'* bodies."

[6] The Caribbean Conference of Churches. At the present time the Catholic Church has full membership in the following national councils of churches: Denmark, Sweden, The Netherlands, Swaziland, Belize, Samoa, Fiji, New Hebrides, Solomon Islands, Papua-New Guinea, Tonga, the Federal Republic of Germany, Botswana, St Vincent, Sudan, Uganda, Finland, Guyana, Trinidad and Tobago.

[7] Minutes of the *Joint Working Group between the Roman Catholic Church and the World Council of Churches* (meeting held in June 1971, Bernhäuser Forst, Stuttgart, Germany), p.10 (unpublished).

[8] In certain cases where Catholic membership in a national council of churches is under consideration, studies have been undertaken and later published. They are of interest as applying general principles to given situations. Examples are: *The Implications of Roman Catholic Membership of the British Council of Churches* (1972), British Council of Churches, London; *Report on Possible Roman Catholic Membership in the National Council of Churches* (1972), US Catholic Conference, Washington; *Groupe mixte de travail — Comité pour de nouvelles structures œcuméniques*, Office national d'œcuménisme, 1452 rue Drummond, Montréal 107.

[9] Cf. *Unitatis Redintegratio*, 1; *Lumen Gentium*, 8,13.

[10] Cf. *Unitatis Redintegratio*, 6.

[11] Cf. *Lumen Gentium, 15; Unitatis Redintegratio*, 3 sqq; etc.

[12] Cf. also *Unitatis Redintegratio*, 4,12; *Apostolicam Actuositatem*, 27.

[13] Cf. *Ecumenical Directory*, Part II, para. 1; "Reflections and Suggestions Concerning Ecumenical Dialogue", II, 2c and d (a working instrument at the disposal of ecclesiastical authorities for concrete application of the Decree on Ecumenism, published in *Information Service* 12 [1970], pp.5-11).

[14] Cf. *Lumen Gentium*, 15; *Unitatis Redintegratio*, 3; also *Minutes and Report of the Third Meeting of the Central Committee, Toronto, Canada, 9-15 July 1950*. The "Toronto Statement", while it refers directly to the World Council of Churches, appears to be fully applicable to similar organizations such as a national council of churches.

[15] *Ibid* ("Toronto Statement").

[16] *Lumen Gentium*, 8.

[17] Synod of Bishops, *Justice in the World*, Typis Polyglottis Vaticanis (1971), p.6; *Documenta Synodi Episcoporum*, De Iustitia in Mundo; *AAS* 63 (1971), p.924.

[18] "And if in moral matters there are many Christians who do not always understand the Gospel in the same way as Catholics and do not admit the same solutions for the more difficult problems of modern society, nevertheless they share our desire to cling to Christ's word as the source of Christian virtue and to obey the apostolic command: 'Whatever you do in word or in work, do all in the name of the Lord Jesus, giving thanks to God the Father through him' (Col. 3:17). Hence, the ecumenical dialogue could start with discussions concerning the application of the Gospel to moral questions" (*Unitatis Redintegratio*, 23, para. 3).

Conferences and Councils in Direct/Indirect Relationship with the WCC

● The information in the following lists is the most up-to-date available at the time of publication. The World Council of Churches corresponds with and sends documents to the conferences and councils and other bodies in the WCC working language indicated below the name.

INDEX

Other bodies (listed by location of headquarters)

Regional Conferences

All Africa Conference of Churches/Conférence des Eglises de toute l'Afrique
(English and French)

General Secretary:
Rev. José Belo Chipenda
P.O. Box 14205, Westlands, Nairobi, Kenya
(Waiyaki Way, Nairobi)

President and Chairman of General Committee:
Most Rev. Desmond Tutu
Archbishop of Capetown
Bishopscourt, Claremont 7700, Cape Province, South Africa

Christian Conference of Asia
(English)

General Secretary:
Rev. PARK Sang Jung
(temporary address)
57 Peking Road (4th floor), Tsim Sha Tsui, Kowloon, Hong Kong

Associate General Secretary:
Rev. Dr A. George Ninan
same address

Caribbean Conference of Churches
(English)

General Secretary:
Rev. Allan F. Kirton
P.O. Box 616, Bridgetown, Barbados, West Indies

Associate General Secretary:
(Programme Planning and Coordination)
same address

Associate General Secretary:
Ms Beryl Carasco
(Human Resources)
same address

Conference of European Churches
(English, French, German)

General Secretary:
Mr Jean Fischer
150 Route de Ferney, P.O.Box 66, 1211 Geneva 20, Switzerland

Chairman:
Metropolitan Alexy of Leningrad and Novgorod

Vice-Chairman:
Very Rev. John Arnold/Dean of Rochester

Consejo Latino Americano de Iglesias (CLAI)/(Latin American Council of Churches)
(Spanish)

General Secretary:
Rev. Felipe Adolf
Casilla 85-22, Quito, Ecuador (Av. Patria 640 y Amazonas, ofc. 1001 Quito)

President:
Bishop Federico Pagura
Rivadavia 4044, 1205 Buenos Aires, Argentina

Middle East Council of Churches
(English)

General Secretary:
Mr Gabriel Habib
(temporary address)
P.O. Box 4259, Limassol, Cyprus

Associate General Secretary:
Dr M. Assad
1127 Corniche El-Nil, Cairo, Egypt

Pacific Conference of Churches
(English and French)

General Secretary:
Mr S. K. Motu'ahala
P.O. Box 208, Suva, Fiji, South Pacific

Chairman:
Rt Rev. Leslie Boseto
P.O. Box 82, Munda, Western Province, Solomon Islands

Associate Councils
of the World Council of Churches

C = Councils also affiliated with the WCC Commission
  on World Mission and Evangelism (CWME)

Australia
(English)

Australian Council of Churches (C)
General Secretary: Rev. David Gill
P.O. Box C 199 Clarence Street, Sydney, NSW 2000, Australia
(379 Kent Street, Sydney)

Austria
(German)

Oekumenischer Rat der Kirchen in Oesterreich
(Ecumenical Council of Churches in Austria)
Vorsitzender: Rev. Dr Ernst Kreuzeder, Lannerstr. 30, A-1191 Vienna, Austria

Botswana
(English)

Botswana Christian Council
General Secretary: Mr N.T.K. Mmono
P.O. Box 355, Gaborone, Botswana

Brazil
(Spanish and English)

Conselho Nacional de Igrejas Cristas do Brasil (CONIC)
(National Council of Christian Churches in Brazil)
Executive Secretary: Rev. Godofredo G. Boll
Caixa Postal 2876, 90.000 Porto Alegre, R.S., Brazil

Burma
(English)

Burma Council of Churches (C)
General Secretary: Rev. Canon Andrew Mya Han
GPO Box 1400, Rangoon, Burma
(Central YMCA Building, 263 Maha Bandoola Street, Rangoon)

Canada
(English and French)

Canadian Council of Churches/Conseil canadien des Eglises (C)
General Secretary: Rev. Dr Donald W. Anderson
40 St Clair Avenue East, Suite 201, Toronto, Ontario M4T lM9, Canada

Cuba
(Spanish)

Consejo Ecuménico de Cuba
(Ecumenical Council of Cuba)
President: Rev. Raúl Suárez Ramos
Apartado 4179, Havana 4, Cuba
(Calle 6 no. 273 e/12 y 13, Vedado, Havana)

Czechoslovakia
(German)

Czechoslovak Ecumenical Council of Churches
General Secretary: Prof. Dr Anezka Ebertova
Vitkova 13, 18600 Praha-Karlin, CSSR

Denmark
(English)

Ecumenical Council of Denmark
Secretary: Mr Peter Lodberg
Norregade 11, DK-1165 Copenhagen K, Denmark

Finland
(English)

Ecumenical Council of Finland (C)
General Secretary: Rev. Jaakko Rusama
Box 185, SF-00161 Helsinki 16, Finland
(Luotsikatu 1a, SF-00160 Helsinki)

The Gambia
(English)

Christian Council of the Gambia
General Secretary: Mr J. Tunde Taylor-Thomas
P.O. Box 27, Banjul, The Gambia, West Africa

German Democratic Republic
(German)

Arbeitsgemeinschaft Christlicher Kirchen in der Deutschen Demokratischen Republik
(Council of Christian Churches in the GDR)
Geschäftsführer: Pastor M. Lange
Auguststrasse 80, DDR-1040 Berlin, German Democratic Republic

Germany, Federal Republic of
(German)

Arbeitsgemeinschaft Christlicher Kirchen in der Bundesrepublik Deutschland und Berlin (West) e.V.
(Council of Christian Churches in the Federal Republic of Germany and West Berlin)
General Secretary: Dr Athanasios Basdekis
Postfach 10 17 62, D-6000 Frankfurt am Main 1, FRG
(Neue Schlesingergasse 22-24, Frankfurt/Main)

Ghana
(English)

Christian Council of Ghana (C)
General Secretary: Rev. Anselm Kofi Zormelo
P.O. Box 919, Accra, Ghana
(Lokko Road, Christiansborg, Accra)

Hong Kong
(English)

Hong Kong Christian Council (C)
General Secretary: Rev. KWOK Nai Wang
33 Granville Road, 9th floor, Tsim Sha Tsui, Kowloon, Hong Kong

Hungary
(German)

Ecumenical Council of Churches in Hungary
General Secretary: Rev. Dr Tibor Goeroeg
Szabadsag 2 1, H-1054 Budapest, Hungary

India
(English)

National Council of Churches in India (C)
General Secretary: Mr Mathai Zachariah
Christian Council Lodge, Civil Lines, Nagpur 440-001, India

Indonesia
(English)

Communion of Churches in Indonesia (C)
General Secretary: Dr Fridolin Ukur
Jalan Salemba Raya 10, Jakarta 10430, Indonesia

Jamaica
(English)

Jamaica Council of Churches
Acting General Secretary: Ms Doreen Kirkcaldy
P.O. Box 30, Kingston 10, Jamaica, West Indies
(14 South Avenue, Kingston)

Japan
(English)

National Christian Council in Japan (C)
General Secretary: Rev. MAEJIMA Munetoshi
Japan Christian Center, 2-3-18-24 Nishiwaseda, Shinjuku-ku, Tokyo 160, Japan

Liberia
(English)

Liberian Council of Churches
Executive Secretary: Ms Imogene M. Collins
P.O. Box 2191, Monrovia, Liberia
(182 Tubman Blvd, Monrovia)

Malaysia
(English)

Council of Churches of Malaysia (C)
General Secretary: Rev. Denis C. Dutton
26 Jalan University, 46200 Petaling Jaya, Selangor, Malaysia

Namibia
(English)

Council of Churches in Namibia
General Secretary: Dr Abisai Shejavali
P.O. Box 41, Windhoek 9000, Namibia
(8 Mont Blanc Street, Windhoek)

Netherlands
(English)

Council of Churches in the Netherlands
General Secretary: Rev. W.R. van der Zee
Kon. Wilhelminalaan 5, NL-3818 HN Amersfoort, Netherlands

New Zealand
(English)

Conference of Churches in Aotearoa-New Zealand (C)
Executive Secretary/Coordinator: Ms Jocelyn Armstrong
P.O. Box 27-264, Wellington, New Zealand
(185 Willis Street, Wellington)

Philippines
(English)

National Council of Churches in the Philippines (C)
General Secretary: Dr Feliciano Carino
P.O. Box 1767, Manila D-406, Philippines
(879 Epifanio de los Santos Avenue, Quezon City)

Poland
(German)

Polish Ecumenical Council
President: Superintendent Adam Kuczma
General Secretary: Rev. Zdzislaw Pawlik
ul. Willowa 1, 00-790 Warsaw, Poland

St Vincent
(English)

St Vincent Christian Council
Executive Secretary: Mr Liley Cato
P.O. Box 445, Kingstown, St Vincent, West Indies
(Melville Street, Kingstown)

Sierra Leone
(English)

United Christian Council of Sierra Leone (C)
General Secretary: Rev. Eustace L. Renner
P.O. Box 404, Freetown, Sierra Leone
(4A Kingharman Road, Brookfields, Freetown)

Singapore
(English)

National Council of Churches, Singapore (C)
President: Mr G. Abisheganaden
Hon. General Secretary: Rev. Sam C.P. Goh
Paza Lebar P.O. Box 80, Singapore 9154

South Africa
(English)

South African Council of Churches (C)
General Secretary: Rev. Frank Chikane
P.O. Box 4921, Johannesburg 2000, South Africa
(Khotso House, 42 de Villiers Street, Johannesburg)

Sri Lanka
(English)

National Christian Council of Sri Lanka (C)
General Secretary: Mr Shirley J.S. Peiris
490/2 Havelock Road, Colombo 6, Sri Lanka

Sudan
(English)

Sudan Council of Churches
General Secretary: Rev. Ezekiel Kutjok
P.O. Box 469, Khartoum, Sudan
(Inter-Church House, Street 35, New Extension, Khartoum)

Swaziland
(English)

Council of Swaziland Churches
General Secretary: Ms Eunice Nokuthula Sowazi
P.O. Box 1095, Manzini, Swaziland

Sweden
(English)

Swedish Ecumenical Council
Secretary: Rev. Rune Forsbeck
Stortorget 3, S-111 29 Stockholm, Sweden

Tanzania
(English)

Christian Council of Tanzania
General Secretary: Rev. Stanford A. Shauri
P.O. Box 372, Dodoma, Tanzania

Tonga
(English)

Tonga National Council of Churches
Executive Secretary: Mr Laitia Fifita
P.O. Box 1205, Nuku'alofa, Tonga, Pacific

United Kingdom and Ireland
(English)

British Council of Churches
General Secretary: Rev. Dr Philip Morgan
Inter-Church House, 35/41 Lower Marsh, Waterloo, London SE1 7RL, United
Kingdom

Council of Churches for Wales
General Secretary: Rev. Noel A. Davies
21 St Helen's Road, 1st floor, Swansea, West Glamorgan, SA1 4AP, Wales,
United Kingdom

United States of America
(English)

National Council of the Churches of Christ in the USA (C)
General Secretary: Rev. Dr Arie R. Brouwer
475 Riverside Drive, Room 880, New York, NY 10115-0050, USA

Yugoslavia
(English)

Ecumenical Council of Churches in Yugoslavia
General Secretary: Deacon Radomir Rakic
Secretariat, Box 182, Belgrade, Yugoslavia

Zambia
(English)

Christian Council of Zambia (C)
Caretaker: Mr Cheleshe
P.O. Box 30315, Lusaka, Zambia
(Church House, Cairo Road, Lusaka)

Zimbabwe
(English)

Zimbabwe Christian Council (C)
General Secretary: Rev. M.C. Kuchera
P.O. Box 3566, Harare, Zimbabwe
(128 Victoria Street, Harare)

Councils in Working Relationship, though not in Association, with the World Council of Churches

Angola
(Spanish)

Conselho Angolano de Igrejas Evangélicas
(Angolan Council of Evangelical Churches)
General Secretary:
C.P. 1659 or 1301, Luanda, People's Rep. of Angola
(Rua Amilcar Cabral no. 182, 1° andar, Luanda)

Antigua
(English)

Antigua Christian Council
President: Rev. Lloyd Kitson
P.O. Box 863, St John's, Antigua, West Indies

Belize
(English)

Belize Christian Council
Executive Secretary: Ms Jas. A. Jeffries
P.O. Box 508, Belize City, Belize, Central America
(149 Allenby Street, Belize City)

Burundi
(French)

Alliance des Eglises protestantes du Burundi
(Alliance of Burundi Protestant Churches)
General Secretary: Pasteur Noé Nzeyimana
B.P. 17, Bujumbura, Burundi

Cameroon
(French)

Fédération des Eglises et missions évangéliques du Cameroun (FEMEC)
(Federation of Protestant Churches and Missions in Cameroon)
Administrative Secretary: Pasteur Grégoire Ambadiang
B.P. 491, Yaoundé, Cameroun

Chile
(Spanish)

Confraternidad Cristiana de Iglesias
(Christian Fellowship of Churches in Chile)
Director: Mr Juan Sepúlveda
P.O. Box 5391, Santiago 3, Chile
(Victoria Subercaseaux 41, Santiago)

China
(English)

China Christian Council
President: Bishop K.H. Ting, 378 Mo Chou Road, Nanjing, China
General Secretary: Bishop Zheng Jieyeh, 169 Yuen Ming Yuan Road,
Shanghai, China
Associate General Secretary: Mr Han Wenzao, 13 Da Jian Yin Xiang,
Nanjing, China

Cook Islands
(English)

Religious Advisory Council of the Cook Islands
General Secretary: Bishop Robin Leamy
P.O. Box 93, Takamoa, Rarotonga, Cook Islands, Pacific

Curaçao
(English)

Curaçao Council of Churches
Executive Secretary: Rev Fr E. G. Stockman
c/o Bisdom Willemstad, Breedestraat, Curaçao, Netherlands Antilles

Fiji
(English)

Fiji Council of Churches
Interim Secretary: Ms Davila Walker
P.O. Box 2300, Government Buildings, Suva, Fiji, Pacific

France
(French)

Fédération protestante de France
(Protestant Federation of France)
President: Pasteur Jacques Stewart
General Secretary: Pasteur Louis Schweitzer
47, rue de Clichy, F-75009 Paris, France

Guyana
(English)

Guyana Council of Churches
Secretary: Mr Michael McCormack
71 Quamina Street, Georgetown, Guyana

Israel
(English)

United Christian Council in Israel
General Secretary: Mr Charles Kopp
P.O. Box 546, Jerusalem 91004, Israel

International Christian Committee in Israel
Chairperson: Dr Sami Geraisy
P.O. Box 304, Nazareth, Israel

Italy
(French)

Federazione delle Chiese Evangeliche in Italia
(Federation of the Protestant Churches in Italy)
President: Rev. Aurelio Sbaffi
Via Firenze 38, I-00184 Rome, Italy

Jerusalem
(English)

International Christian Committee and Jerusalem Inter-Church Aid Committee
Secretary: Mr Elias Khouri
P.O. Box 19195, Jerusalem

Kenya
(English)

National Council of Churches of Kenya
General Secretary: Rev. Samuel Kobia
P.O. Box 45009, Nairobi, Kenya
(Church House, Moi Avenue, Nairobi)

Lesotho
(English)

Christian Council of Lesotho
General Secretary: Fr Ramolulela Michael Taole
P.O. Box 547, Maseru 100, Lesotho, Southern Africa

Madagascar
(French)

Conseil chrétien des Eglises de Madagascar
(Christian Council of Churches in Madagascar)
General Secretary: Rev. Lala Andriamiharisoa
B.P. 798, 101 Antananarivo, Madagascar
(Vohipiraisama, Ambohijatovo-Atsimo, Antananarivo)

Morocco
(French)

Conseil des Eglises du Maroc
(Council of Churches of Morocco)
33 rue d'Azilal, Casablanca, Morocco

Mozambique
(Spanish)

Conselho Cristao de Mocambique
(Christian Council of Mozambique)
General Secretary: Rev. Felipe Sique Banze
C.P. 108, Maputo, Mozambique
(Ave. Afonso de Albuquerque 1822, Maputo)

New Zealand
(English)

Te Runanga Whakawhanaunga I Nga Hahi O Aotearoa
(Maori Council of Churches in New Zealand)
General Secretary: Rev. Rua Rakena
P.O. Box 9573, Newmarket, Auckland, New Zealand

Nigeria
(English)

Christian Council of Nigeria
General Secretary: Mr C. O. Williams
P.O. Box 2838, Marina, Lagos, Nigeria
(139 Ogunluna Drive, Surulere, Lagos)

Papua New Guinea
(English)

Melanesian Council of Churches
General Secretary: Rev. Leva Kila Pat
Box 1015, Boroko, Port Moresby, Papua New Guinea

Rwanda
(French)

Conseil protestant du Rwanda
(Protestant Council of Rwanda)
General Secretary: Mr Jean Utumbahutu
B.P. 79, Kigali, Rwanda

Samoa
(English)

American Samoa Council of Christian Churches
General Secretary: Rev. Enoka L. Alesana
c/o CCCAS Offices, P.O. Box 1537, Pago Pago, American Samoa 96799, Pacific

Samoa Council of Churches
Secretary: Rev. Oka Fau'olo
P.O. Box 574, Apia, Western Samoa, Pacific

Solomon Islands
(English)

Solomon Islands Christian Association
Secretary: Rev. Philemon Riti
P.O. Box 556, Honiara, Solomon Islands, Pacific

Spain
(Spanish)

Federación de Entidades Religiosas Evangélicas de España
(Spanish Federation of Religious Organizations)
Executive Secretary: Mr José Cardona Gregori
c/o Princesa, 3 Dpdo. no. 1308, E-28008 Madrid, Spain

United Kingdom and Ireland
(English)

Isle of Man Council of Churches
Secretary: Rev. Douglas V. Brown
The Homestead, Bay View Road, Port Erin, Isle of Man, UK

Scottish Churches Council
General Secretary: Rev. Canon Kenyon E. Wright
Scottish Churches' House, Kirk Street,
Dunblane, Perthshire FK15 OAJ, Scotland, UK

Vanuatu
(English)

Vanuatu Christian Council
Secretary: Rev. Allen Nafuki
P.O. Box 379, Port Vila, Vanuatu, Pacific

Zaïre
(French)

Eglise du Christ au Zaïre (member church)
(Church of Christ in Zaïre)
President: Mgr I.B. Bokeleale
B.P. 4938, Kinshasa-Gombe, Zaïre

Affiliated Bodies of the
Conference on World Mission and Evangelism (CWME)

C = Councils of churches affiliated to CWME
M = Mission bodies affiliated to CWME
R = Regional body affiliated to CWME

Argentina
(Spanish)

Federación Argentina de Iglesias Evangélicas (C)
(Argentine Federation of Evangelical Churches)
President: Rev. Rodolfo Reinich
José Maria Moreno 873, 1424 Buenos Aires, Argentina

Australia
(English)

Australian Council of Churches: Commission on Mission (M,C)
General Secretary: Rev. David Gill
P.O. Box C 199 Clarence Street, Sydney, NSW 2000, Australia
(379 Kent Street, Sydney)

Austria
(German)

Oesterreichischer Missionsrat (M)
(Austrian Missionary Council)
Moderator: Dr Julius Hanak
Engerthstrasse 226, A-1024 Vienna, Austria

Bahamas
(English)

Bahamas Christian Council (C)
Secretary: Rev. Charles A. Sweeting
P.O. Box SS-5863, Shirley Street P.O., Nassau, Bahamas, West Indies

Bangladesh
(English)

National Council of Churches, Bangladesh (C)
General Secretary-in-Charge: Mr Subodh Adhikary
P.O. Box 220, Dhaka 2, Bangladesh
(395 New Eskaton Road, Dhaka)

Belgium
(French)

Commission missionnaire de l'Eglise protestante unie de Belgique (M)
(Missionary Commission of the United Protestant Church of Belgium)
President: Mr Marc Lombart
Champ de Mars 5, B-1050 Brussels, Belgium

Burma
(English)

Burma Council of Churches (C)
General Secretary: Rev. Canon Andrew Mya Han
P.O. Box 1400, Rangoon, Burma
(Central YMCA Building, 263 Maha Bandoola Street, Rangoon)

Canada
(English and French)

Canadian Council of Churches/Conseil Canadien des Eglises (C)
General Secretary: Rev. Dr Donald W. Anderson
40 St Clair Avenue East, Suite 201, Toronto, Ontario M4T 1M9, Canada

Cuba
(Spanish)

Consejo Ecuménico de Cuba (C)
(Ecumenical Council of Cuba)
President: Rev. Raúl Suárez Ramos
Apartado 4179, Havana 4, Cuba
(Calle 6 no. 273 e/12 y 13, Vedado, Havana)

Denmark
(English)

Danish Missionary Council (M)
General Secretary: Mr Flemming Kramp
Sankt Lukas Vej, DK-2900 Hellerup, Denmark

Finland
(English)

Ecumenical Council of Finland: Commission on World Mission and
Evangelism (C)
General Secretary: Rev. Jaako Rusama
Luotsikatu 1a, PL 185, SF-00161 Helsinki 16, Finland

France
(French)

Département évangelique français d'action apostolique — Service protestant de
mission et de relations internationales (M)
(French Evangelical Department for Apostolic Action)
General Secretary: Rev. Jean-François Zorn
102 Boulevard Arago, F-75014 Paris, France

German Democratic Republic
(German)

Oekumenisch-Missionarischer Verbindungsausschuss (M)
(Ecumenical Missionary Liaison Committee)
Moderator: Kirchenpräsident Eberhard Natho
Auguststrasse 80, DDR-1040 Berlin, German Democratic Republic

Germany, Federal Republic of
(German)

Evangelisches Missionswerk im Bereich der Bundesrepublik Deutschland und
Berlin (West) e.V. (M)
(Protestant Association for World Mission in the Federal Republic of Germany
and West Berlin)
Director:
Mittelweg 143, D-2000 Hamburg 13, Federal Republic of Germany

Ghana
(English)

Christian Council of Ghana (C)
General Secretary: Rev. Anselm Kofi Zormelo
P.O. Box 919, Accra, Ghana
(Lokko Road, Christiansborg, Accra)

Hong Kong
(English)

Hong Kong Christian Council (C)
General Secretary: Rev. KWOK Nai Wang
33 Granville Road, 9th floor, Tsim Sha Tsui, Kowloon, Hong Kong

India
(English)

National Council of Churches in India (C)
General Secretary: Mr Mathai Zachariah
Christian Council Lodge, Civil Lines, Nagpur 440-001, India

Indonesia
(English)

Communion of Churches in Indonesia (C)
General Secretary: Dr Fridolin Ukur
Jalan Salemba Raya 10, Jakarta 10430, Indonesia

Jamaica
(English)

Jamaica Council of Churches (C)
Acting General Secretary: Ms Doreen Kirkcaldy
P.O. Box 30, Kingston 10, Jamaica, West Indies
(14 South Avenue, Kingston)

Japan
(English)

National Christian Council in Japan (C)
General Secretary: Rev. MAEJIMA Munetoshi
Japan Christian Center, 2-3-18-24 Nishiwaseda, Shinjuku-ku, Tokyo 160, Japan

Korea
(English)

National Council of Churches in Korea (C)
General Secretary:
Kwang-Wha-Moon P.O. Box 134, Seoul, Korea
(Christian Bldg, 136-46 Yonchi-Dong, Chongro-Ku, Seoul 110)

Madagascar
(French)

Fédération des Eglises protestantes à Madagascar (C)
(Federation of the Protestant Churches in Madagascar)
General Secretary: Rev. Charles Rakotoson
V.K.2, Vohipiraisana, Ambohijatovo-Atsimo, 101 Antanarivo, Madagascar

Malawi
(English)

Christian Council of Malawi (C)
General Secretary: Rev. Maxwell Maputwa
P.O. Box 30068, Lilongwe 3, Malawi

Malaysia
(English)

Council of Churches of Malaysia (C)
General Secretary: Rev. Denis C. Dutton
26 Jalan University, Petaling Jaya, Selangor, Malaysia

Mexico
(Spanish)

Federación Evangélica de México (C)
(Evangelical Federation of Mexico)
Executive Secretary: Rev. I. Ortiz Murrieta
Apartado 1830, Mexico 06.001, D.F., Mexico
(Motolinia no. 8-107, Mexico 06.002, D.F.)

Netherlands
(English)

Nederlands Missionary Council (M)
General Secretary: Rev. Jan van Butselaar
37 Prins Hendriklaan, NL-1075 BA Amsterdam, Netherlands

New Zealand
(English)

Conference of Churches in Aotearoa-New Zealand (C)
Executive Secretary/Coordinator: Ms Jocelyn Armstrong
P.O. Box 27-264, Wellington, New Zealand
(185 Willis Street, Wellington)

Pakistan
(English)

National Council of Churches in Pakistan (C)
Executive Secretary: Mr William K. Mall
P.O. Box 357, Lahore 4, Pakistan
(32-B Shar-e-Fatima Jinnah, Lahore)

Philippines
(English)

National Council of Churches in the Philippines (C)
General Secretary: Dr Feliciano Carino
P.O. Box 1767, Manila D-406, Philippines
(879 Epifanio de los Santos Avenue, Quezon City)

Portugal
(English)

Conselho Portugues de Igrejas Cristas (C)
(Portuguese Council of Christian Churches)
General Secretary: Rev. Manuel Pedro Cardoso
Rua da Lapa 9, sala 1, 2º andar, P-3080 Figueira da Foz, Portugal

Puerto Rico
(Spanish)

Concilio Evangélico de Puerto Rico (C)
(Evangelical Council of Puerto Rico)
General Secretary: Dr Rubén Pérez Torres
Apartado Postal 21343, Rio Piedras, Puerto Rico 00928

Sierra Leone
(English)

United Christian Council of Sierra Leone (C)
General Secretary: Rev. Eustace L. Renner
P.O. Box 404, Freetown, Sierra Leone
(4A Kingharman Road, Brookfields, Freetown)

Singapore
(English)

National Council of Churches, Singapore (C)
President: Mr G. Abisheganaden
Hon.General Secretary: Rev. V.E. Thomas
14 Dalvey Estate, Singapore 1025

South Africa
(English)

South African Council of Churches (C)
General Secretary: Rev. Frank Chikane
P.O. Box 4921, Johannesburg 2000, South Africa
(Khotso House, 42 de Villiers Street, Johannesburg)

Sri Lanka
(English)

National Christian Council of Sri Lanka (C)
General Secretary: Mr Shirley J.S. Peiris
490/2 Havelock Road, Colombo 6, Sri Lanka

Sweden
(English)

Swedish Missionary Council (M)
Secretary: Rev. Per Ake Wahlström
Götgatan 3, 1 tr., S-752 22 Uppsala, Sweden

Switzerland
(German and French)

Schweizerischer Evangelischer Missionsrat — Conseil suisse des missions évangeliques (M)
(Swiss Protestant Missionary Council)
Secretary: Mr Roland Dumartheray
Hohmüedig 17, CH-3800 Unterseen-Interlaken, Switzerland

Thailand
(English)

Church of Christ in Thailand (member church)
General Secretary: Rev. Boonratna Boayen
14 Pramuan Road, Bangkok 10500, Thailand

Trinidad and Tobago
(English)

Christian Council of Trinidad and Tobago (C)
Executive Secretary: Ms Grace Steele
Hayes Court, Hayes Street, Port-of-Spain, Trinidad and Tobago, West Indies

United Kingdom and Ireland
(English)

Conference for World Mission (M)
General Secretary: Rev. Dr Fergus Macpherson
Inter-Church House, 35-41 Lower Marsh, Waterloo, London SE1 7RL, United Kingdom

Irish Council of Churches (C)
General Secretary: Rt Hon. David W. Bleakley
48 Elmwood Avenue, Belfast BT9 6AZ, Northern Ireland, United Kingdom

United States of America
(English)

National Council of the Churches of Christ in the USA (C)
General Secretary: Rev. Dr Arie R. Brouwer
475 Riverside Drive, New York, NY 10115-0050, USA

Joint Strategy and Action Committee (M)
Executive Director: Rev. John C. DeBoer
475 Riverside Drive, Suite 450, New York, NY 10115-0050, USA

Uruguay
(Spanish)

Federación de Iglesias Evangélicas del Uruguay (C)
(Federation of Evangelical Churches of Uruguay)
Executive Secretary: Mr Lothar Driedger
Av. 8 de octubre 3324, Montevideo, Uruguay

Zaïre
(French)

Eglise de Jésus-Christ sur la terre par le prophète Simon Kimbangu (member church)
(Church of Jesus Christ on Earth by the Prophet Simon Kimbangu)
Spiritual Leader: His Eminence Diangienda-Kuntima
P.O. Box 7069, Kinshasa 1, Zaïre

Zambia
(English)

Christian Council of Zambia (C)
Caretaker: Mr Cheleshe
P.O. Box 30315, Lusaka, Zambia
(Church House, Cairo Road, Lusaka)

Zimbabwe
(English)

Zimbabwe Christian Council (C)
General Secretary: Rev. M.C. Kuchera
P.O. Box 3566, Harare, Zimbabwe
(128 Victoria Street, Harare)

Regional Bodies

Communauté évangélique d'action apostolique (CEVAA) (M)
(Evangelical Community for Apostolic Action)
General Secretary: Pasteur Samuel Ada
12, rue de Miromesnil, F-75008 Paris, France

Council for World Mission (M)
General Secretary: Dr Christopher Duraisingh
Livingstone House, 11 Carteret Street, London SW1H 9DL, UK

Middle East Council of Churches (R)
General Secretary: Mr Gabriel Habib
P.O. Box 4259, Limassol, Cyprus
(temporary address)

Bodies having a consultative relationship with CWME

White Fathers
Rev. Jan Lenssen, P.A.
Via Aurelia 269, I-00165 Rome, Italy

Order of Don Bosco (Salesians)
Rev. Father Antonio Smit, SDB
Dodeweg 6, NL-3832 RC Leusden, Netherlands

Sisters of the Catholic Apostolate
Revd Sister Clementia Burkard, SAC
Viale delle Mure Aurelie, 7/B, I-00165 Rome, Italy

Marist Missionary Sisters
Sister Patricia Stowers, smsm
Via Cassia 1243, I-00189 Rome, Italy

Participants

The position indicated is that held by the participant at the time of the consultation. Addresses are given only where they are not to be found in Appendix 2. The personal confessional affiliation is given in parentheses.

Mr Michael Sushil ADHIKARI (Baptist)
President, National Council of Churches, Bangladesh

Rev. Dr Grégoire AMBADIANG (Reformed)
Administrative Secretary, Federation of Protestant Churches and Missions in Cameroon

Rev. Dr Donald W. ANDERSON (Anglican)
General Secretary, Canadian Council of Churches

Rev. Canon Lala ANDRIAMIHARISOA (Anglican)
General Secretary, Christian Council of Churches in Madagascar

Ms Jocelyn ARMSTRONG (Anglican)
General Secretary, National Council of Churches in New Zealand

Dr Trond BAKKEVIG (Lutheran)
General Secretary, Council on Foreign Relations, Church of Norway, P.O. Box 5816, Hegdehaugen, 0308 Oslo 3, Norway

Rev. Martin J. BEUKENHORST (United)
President, United Protestant Church of Belgium, Rue du Champ-de-Mars 5, 1050 Brussels, Belgium

Rev. Dr Alexei BICHKOV (Baptist)
General Secretary, All Union of Evangelical Christians — Baptists of USSR,
G.P.O. Box 520, Moscow, USSR

Mr T. Makanya BITA (Roman Catholic)
Director of Development Services, Christian Council of Tanzania

Rt Hon. David W. BLEAKLEY (Anglican)
General Secretary, Irish Council of Churches

Mgr BOKELEALE (Disciples)
President, Church of Christ in Zaire

Rev. Godofredo G. BOLL (Lutheran)
Executive Secretary, National Council of Christian Churches in Brazil (CONIC)

Ms Gunnel BORGEGARD (Free Church)
Assistant General Secretary, Swedish Ecumenical Council

Rev. Dr Arie R. BROUWER (Reformed)
General Secretary, National Council of the Churches of Christ in the USA

Rev. Manuel Pedro CARDOSO (Reformed)
General Secretary, Portuguese Council of Christian Churches (COPIC)

Rev. José B. CHIPENDA (Reformed)
General Secretary, Angolan Council of Evangelical Churches

Rev. Dr Saindi CHIPHANGWI (Reformed)
Chairman, Christian Council of Malawi

Rev. Pierre CHRETIEN (Lutheran)
General Secretary, Protestant Federation of France

Prof. Dr Dan Ilie CIOBOTEA (Orthodox)
Lecturer, Ecumenical Institute, Bossey, 1298 Céligny, Switzerland
representing the Romanian Orthodox Church

Bishop Edgerton CLARKE (Roman Catholic)
Vice President, Jamaica Council of Churches

Ms Imogene M. COLLINS (Baptist)
General Secretary, Liberian Council of Churches

Rev. Theodorus A. DARNOUD (Moravian)
President, Surinam Council of Churches

Rev. Noel A. DAVIES (Congregational)
General Secretary, Council of Churches for Wales

Rev. Denis C. DUTTON (Methodist)
General Secretary, Council of Churches of Malaysia

Prof. Dr Anezka EBERTOVA (Hussite)
General Secretary, Czechoslovak Ecumenical Council of Churches

Mr Don EDKINS
General Secretary, Christian Council of Lesotho

Rev. Rune FORSBECK (Reformed)
General Secretary, Swedish Ecumenical Council

Dr Johannes GARANG (Reformed)
Secretary, Department of Research and Study, Communion of Churches in
Indonesia

Sr Donna GEERNAERT (Roman Catholic)
Member of the Board, Canadian Council of Churches

Dr Sami Farah GERAISY (Orthodox)
Chairman of the Board of Directors, International Christian Committee in Israel
representing the Middle East Council of Churches

Rev. David GILL (United)
General Secretary, Uniting Church in Australia,
P.O. Box E266, St James 2000, NSW, Australia
representing the Australian Council of Churches

Rev. Dr Tibor GOEROEG (Lutheran)
General Secretary, Ecumenical Council of Churches in Hungary

Mr Gabriel HABIB (Orthodox)
General Secretary, Middle East Council of Churches

Metropolitan G. Yohanna IBRAHIM (Orthodox)
Archbishop of Aleppo, Syrian Orthodox Church
representing the Middle East Council of Churches

Rev. Clement H. JANDA (Anglican)
General Secretary, Sudan Council of Churches

Pastor Jean-Pierre JORNOD (Reformed)
General Secretary, Swiss Protestant Church Federation

Rev. Stylianos KALOTERAKIS (Reformed)
Konst. Paleologou 6, 546 22 Thessaloniki, Greece
representing the Greek Evangelical Church

Mr John C. KAMAU (Reformed)
General Secretary, National Council of Churches of Kenya

Rev. Allan F. KIRTON (Methodist)
General Secretary, Caribbean Conference of Churches

Dr Laurentius KLEIN, OSB (Roman Catholic)
General Secretary, Council of Christian Churches in the Federal Republic of
Germany and West Berlin

Dr Elfriede KREUZEDER
Vice President, Ecumenical Council of Churches in Austria

Rev. Murombedzi C. KUCHERA (United)
General Secretary, Zimbabwe Christian Council

Pastor Martin LANGE (Methodist)
General Secretary, Council of Christian Churches in the German Democratic
Republic

Prof. Hervé LEGRAND, O.P. (Roman Catholic)
Couvent St Jacques, Rue de Tanneries 20, 75013 Paris, France
representing the Secretariat for Promoting Christian Unity of the Roman Catholic
Church

Dr Lorand LENGYEL (Reformed)
Stefan Mora Str. 7, 3400 Cluj-Napoca, Romania
representing the Reformed Church of Romania

Ms Eileen LINDNER (Reformed)
Assistant General Secretary for Planning and Programme Development, National
Council of the Churches of Christ in the USA

Mr Peter LODBERG (Lutheran)
General Secretary, Ecumenical Council of Denmark

Bishop José Ivo LORSCHEITER (Roman Catholic)
President, National Council of Christian Churches in Brazil (CONIC)

Rev. LUNTADILA Ndala Za Fwa (Kimbanguist)
General Secretary, Church of Jesus Christ on Earth by the Prophet Simon
Kimbangu, P.O. Box 11375, Bongolo, Kinshasa I, Zaire

Rev. MAEJIMA Munetoshi (United)
General Secretary, National Christian Council in Japan

Mr Ben MASILO (Reformed)
Acting Secretary, Human Rights Commission, All Africa Conference of
Churches

Rev. Jacques MAURY (Reformed)
President, Protestant Federation of France

Mr Michael McCORMACK (Roman Catholic)
Secretary, Guyana Council of Churches

Mgr Basil MEEKING (Roman Catholic)
Under-Secretary, Secretariat for Promoting Christian Unity, 00120 Vatican City

Rev. Albino MELENDEZ OBANDO (Baptist)
P.O. Box 3091, Managua, Nicaragua
representing the Evangelical Committee for Development Aid (CEPAD)

Bishop La Verne D. MERCADO (Methodist)
General Secretary, National Council of Churches in the Philippines

Mr Nathaniel T.K. MMONO
General Secretary, Botswana Christian Council

Rev. Carlos MORALES (United)
President, Permanent Commission of the Spanish Evangelical Church,
Estación Chilches, Los Rubios (Málaga), Spain

Rev. Dr Philip MORGAN (United)
General Secretary, British Council of Churches

Ms Marion MORGAN (Roman Catholic)
Executive Secretary, Bristol Council of Churches (UK)
representing the Secretariat for Promoting Christian Unity of the Roman Catholic
Church

Mr Sione K.F. MOTU'AHALA (Methodist)
Executive Secretary, Tonga National Council of Churches

Rev. John MUTISO-MBINDA (Roman Catholic)
Secretariat for Promoting Christian Unity, 00120 Vatican City

Rev. Canon Andrew MYA HAN (Anglican)
General Secretary, Burma Council of Churches

Rev. Dr C.F. Beyers NAUDÉ (Reformed)
General Secretary, South African Council of Churches

Mgr Samuel NDAYISENGA
representing the Alliance of Burundi Protestant Churches

Bishop Louis N. NDLOVU (Roman Catholic)
Chairman, Council of Swaziland Churches

Rev. Kjell O. NILSSON (Lutheran)
Director, Nordic Ecumenical Institute, P.O. Box 438, 751 06 Uppsala, Sweden

Rev. Bernhard NORDKAMP (Roman Catholic)
representing the Council of Churches in Namibia

Rev. Canon Charles OBAIKOL-EBITU (Anglican)
Provincial Secretary, Church of Uganda
P.O. Box 14123, Kampala, Uganda

Rev. Israel ORTIZ MURRIETA (Pentecostal)
Exexutive Secretary, Evangelical Federation of Mexico

Mr Cees OSKAM (Reformed)
Director of Projects, Interchurch Coordination Committee for Development
Projects, P.O. Box 151, 3700 AD Zeist, Netherlands

Rev. PARK Sang Jung (Holiness)
General Secretary, Christian Conference of Asia

Rev. Leva K. PAT (United)
Caretaker General Secretary, Melanesian Council of Churches

Mr Shirley J.S. PEIRIS (Anglican)
General Secretary, National Christian Council of Sri Lanka

Rev. Horacio PRADO (Independent)
President, Evangelical Fellowship of Ecuador, P.O. Box 3798, Quito, Ecuador

Rev. Maxime V. RAFRANSOA (United)
General Secretary, All Africa Conference of Churches

Rev. Tomasi RAIKIVI (Methodist)
General Secretary, Fiji Council of Churches

Rev. Charles RAKOTOSON (Lutheran)
General Secretary, Federation of the Protestant Churches in Madagascar

Rev. Luther Zwingli RAPRAP (Reformed)
Secretary of the Department on Unity, Evangelism and Church Renewal,
Communion of Churches in Indonesia

Rev. Eustace L. RENNER (Methodist)
General Secretary, United Christian Council of Sierra Leone

Rev. Lal RINMAWIA (Reformed)
Secretary of Unit II (Evangelistic and Social Mission), National Council of
Churches in India

Rev. Philemon RITI (United)
General Secretary, Solomon Islands Christian Association

Rev. Juan Marcos RIVERA (Disciples)
Executive Secretary, Evangelical Council of Puerto Rico

Fr Gysbertus Johannes ROEST (Roman Catholic)
Van Rensselaerstraat 1, 3862 Am Nijkerk, Surinam
representing the Surinam Council of Churches

Sr Luis Aurelio ROSSO DROZ (Methodist)
President, Federation of Evangelical Churches of Uruguay

Rev. Jaakko RUSAMA (Lutheran)
General Secretary, Ecumenical Council of Finland

Rev. Philip SAUNDERS (Methodist)
Vice Chairman, Christian Council of Trinidad and Tobago

Rev. Juan SEPULVEDA (Pentecostal)
President, Christian Fellowship of Churches in Chile

Bishop SERGIY OF SOLNECHOGORSK (Orthodox)
Representative of the Moscow Patriarchate of the Russian Orthodox Church,
Ecumenical Centre, P.O. Box 66, 1211 Geneva 20, Switzerland

Dr Abisai SHEJAVALI (Lutheran)
General Secretary, Council of Churches in Namibia

Rev. Dr G.R. SINGH (Methodist)
Secretary of Unit I (Fellowship, Dialogue and Unity), National Council of
Churches in India

Rev. Felipe SIQUE BANZE
General Secretary, Christian Council of Mozambique

Ms Jean SKUSE (United)
General Secretary, Australian Council of Churches

Ms Eunice Nokuthula SOWAZI (Roman Catholic)
General Secretary, Council of Swaziland Churches

Rev. Blanca STAUDE DE MARTINEZ (Disciples)
Secretary, Argentine Federation of Evangelical Churches

Mr Francis STEPHANOS (Lutheran)
President, Ethiopian Evangelical Church Mekane Yesus,
P.O. Box 2087, Addis Ababa, Ethiopia

Mr John SULEMAN (United)
Member of the Executive Committee, National Council of Churches in Pakistan

Senior Jan SZAREK (Lutheran)
Moderator of the Commission on Interchurch Aid, Polish Ecumenical Council

Rev. Talelelei TAPU (Anglican)
Member of the Steering Committee, Samoa Council of Churches

Mr J. Tunde TAYLOR-THOMAS (Anglican)
Secretary General, Christian Council of the Gambia

Bishop Benedict To VARPIN (Roman Catholic)
Chairman of Catholic Bishops' Commission for Ecumenism,
c/o P.O. Box 1015, Boroko, NCD, Papua New Guinea
representing the Melanesian Council of Churches

Rev. Jean UTUMABAHUTU (Reformed)
General Secretary, Protestant Council of Rwanda

Prof. Christos VOULGARIS (Orthodox)
Member of the Synodical Committee on Inter-Orthodox and Interchurch Relations, Church of Greece, 16 Eptanisou Street, 152 31 Halandrion, Greece

Mr Charles O. WILLIAMS (Methodist)
General Secretary, Christian Council of Nigeria

Dr Glen Garfield WILLIAMS (Baptist)
General Secretary, Conference of European Churches

Rev. Bertrice WOOD (United)
Member of the Governing Board, National Council of the Churches of Christ in the USA

Rev. Canon Kenyon E. WRIGHT (Anglican)
General Secretary, Scottish Churches Council

L.M. Abebaw YEGZAW (Orthodox)
General Secretary, Ethiopian Orthodox Church,
P.O. Box 1283, Addis Ababa, Ethiopia

Rev. Dr Rupert A. YOUNG (Methodist)
Assistant Secretary, Jamaica Council of Churches

Rev. W.R. van der ZEE (Reformed)
General Secretary, Council of Churches in the Netherlands

Rev. Anselm Kofi ZORMELO (Methodist)
General Secretary, Christian Council of Ghana

WCC staff

Rev. Dr Samuel AMIRTHAM
  (United)
Rev. Tosh ARAI (United)
Rev. Wesley ARIARAJAH
  (Methodist)
Ms Marie ASSAAD (Orthodox)
Ms Jane BACK-DUNCAN (Anglican)
Mr Huibert van BEEK (Reformed)
Mr Pierre BEFFA (Roman Catholic)
Ms Midge BEGUIN-AUSTIN
  (Disciples)
Dr Ans van der BENT (United)
Ms Anne BERGER-WILLIAMSON
  (Reformed)
Rev. Dr Thomas BEST (Disciples)
Ms Margrit BISCHOF
  (Roman Catholic)
Ms Brigitte BOTROS (Reformed)
Dr Stuart BROWN (Anglican)
Ms Auriol BURROWS (United)
Rev. Joan CAMPBELL (Disciples)
Rev. Dr Emilio CASTRO (Methodist)
Ms Eileen CHAPMAN (United)
Mr Patrick COIDAN (Reformed)
Sr Joan DELANEY (Roman Catholic)
Mr Michael DOMINGUEZ (Disciples)
Ms Andrée DURAND (Reformed)
Ms Nicole FISCHER (Reformed)
Mr Raymond FUNG (Baptist)
Prof. Dr Adriaan GEENSE
  (Reformed)
Mr Uffe GJERDING (Lutheran)
Ms Rosemary GREEN (United)
Ms Erna HALLER (Reformed)
Rev. Anna Karin HAMMAR
  (Lutheran)
Rev. Charles HARPER (Reformed)
Ms Anneliese HOPPE (Lutheran)
Mr André JACQUES (Reformed)
Ms Lynda KATSUNO (United)
Ms Katie KELLER (Anglican)
Mr Melaku KIFLE (Orthodox)
Mr Tad MITSUI (United)

Rev. Ofelia ORTEGA-MONTOYA
  (Reformed)
Ms Priscilla PADOLINA (Methodist)
Ms Marta PALMA (Pentecostal)
Dr PARK Kyung Seo (Reformed)
Rev. William PERKINS (Anglican)
Dr Klaus POSER (United)
Ms Caroline REUVER
  (Roman Catholic)
Dr Ghassan RUBEIZ (Orthodox)
Prof. Todor SABEV (Orthodox)
Ms Heidi SCHWEIZER (Reformed)
Rev. Carlos SINTADO (Methodist)
Ms Thelma SKILLER (United)
Ms Gudrun SMITH (Lutheran)
Ms Ruth SOVIK (Lutheran)
Rev. Eugene STOCKWELL
  (Methodist)
Mr Lal SWAI (Lutheran)
Ms Lorine TEVI (Methodist)
Mr Marlin VANELDEREN
  (Reformed)
Mr Erich WEINGARTNER (Lutheran)

Interpreters
Ms Beatriz ATENCIO
Ms Hilde BENZ
Ms Manuela BROWN
Ms Fernanda COMBA
Ms Pilar DELARAYE
Ms Christine DEMONT
Ms Tomoko EVDOKIMOFF
Ms Linda MENCHI
Ms Alice NEMEC
Mr Charles ODIER
Ms Ursula ZIERL

Contributors

Ms *Ruth Sovik* is deputy general secretary of the WCC and moderator of its programme unit II.

Mr *Marlin VanElderen* is editor of the WCC's monthly magazine, *One World*.

The Rev. Dr *Thomas F. Best* is executive secretary with the WCC's Commission on Faith and Order.

The Rev. *Allan F. Kirton* is general secretary of the Caribbean Conference of Churches.

Prof. *Hervé Legrand, O.P.* is professor at the Catholic Institute of Paris.

Prof. Dr *Anezka Ebertova* is general secretary of the Czechoslovak Ecumenical Council of Churches.

Bishop *La Verne D. Mercado* was general secretary of the National Council of Churches in the Philippines.

Ms *Jean Skuse* was general secretary of the Australian Council of Churches. She is now executive officer for Australian preparation for the WCC Seventh Assembly, Canberra, 1991.

The Rev. *Godofredo G. Boll* is executive secretary of the National Council of Christian Churches in Brazil.

The Rev. Dr *C.F. Beyers Naudé* was general secretary of the South African Council of Churches.